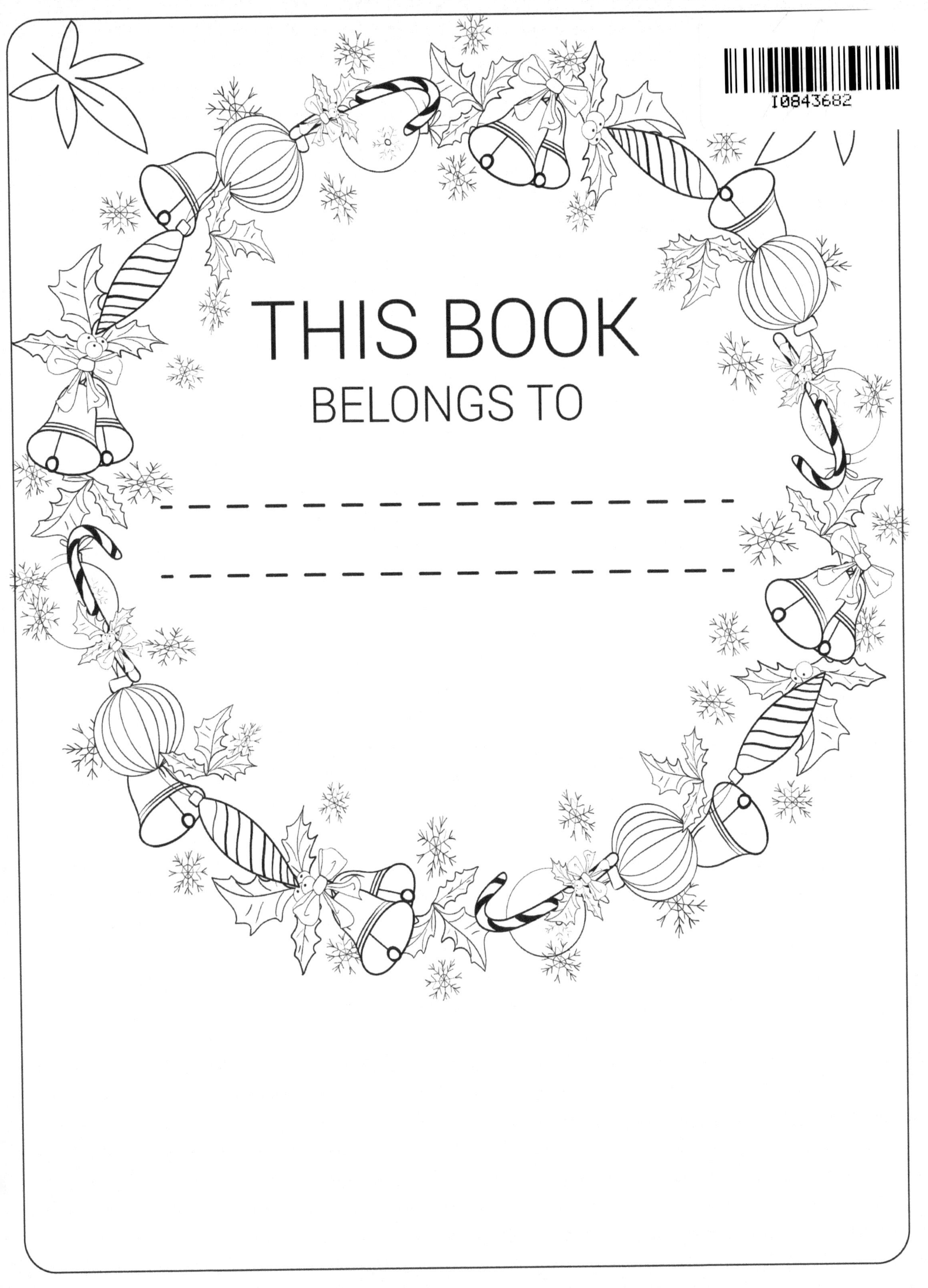

THIS BOOK
BELONGS TO

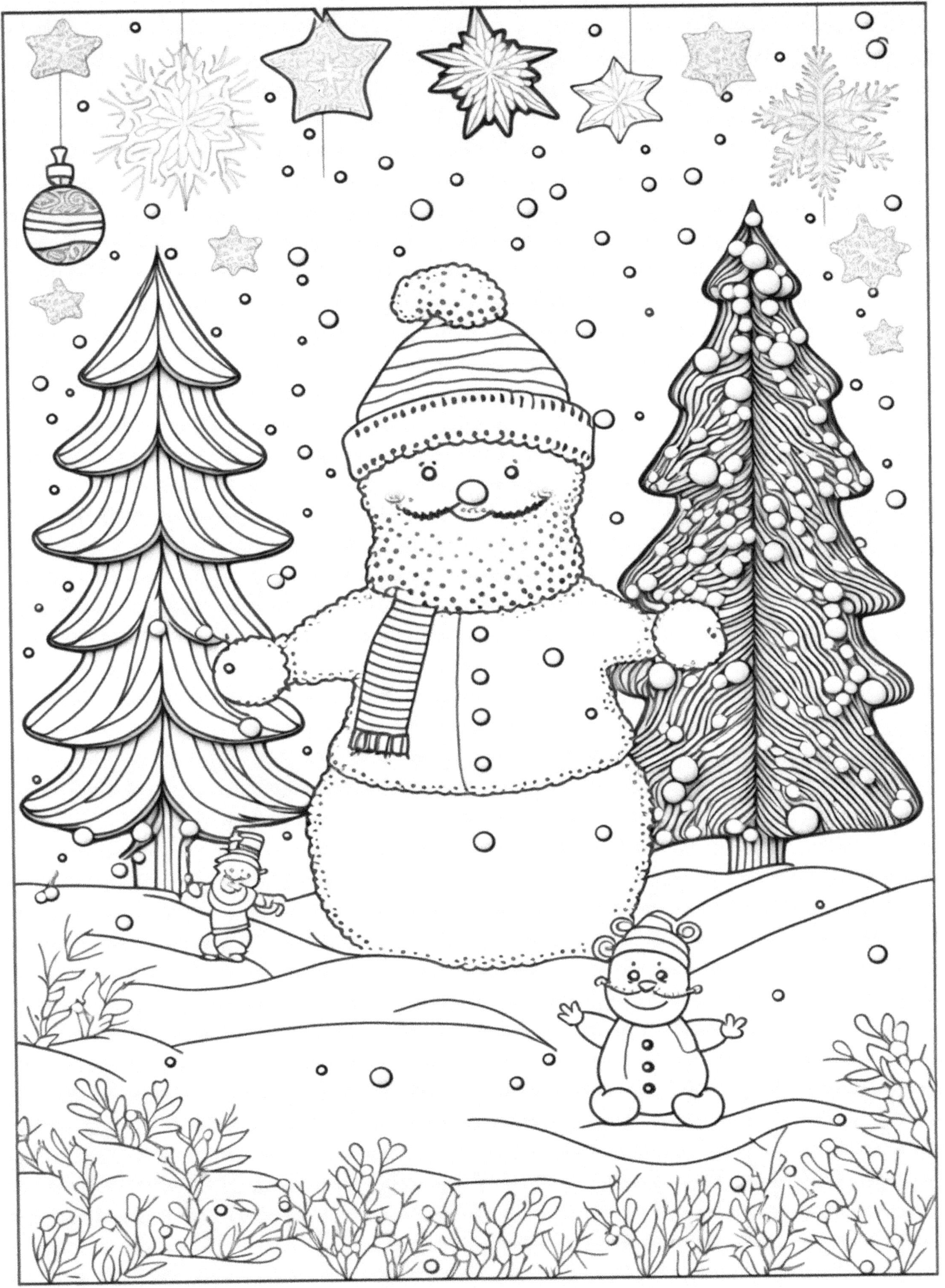

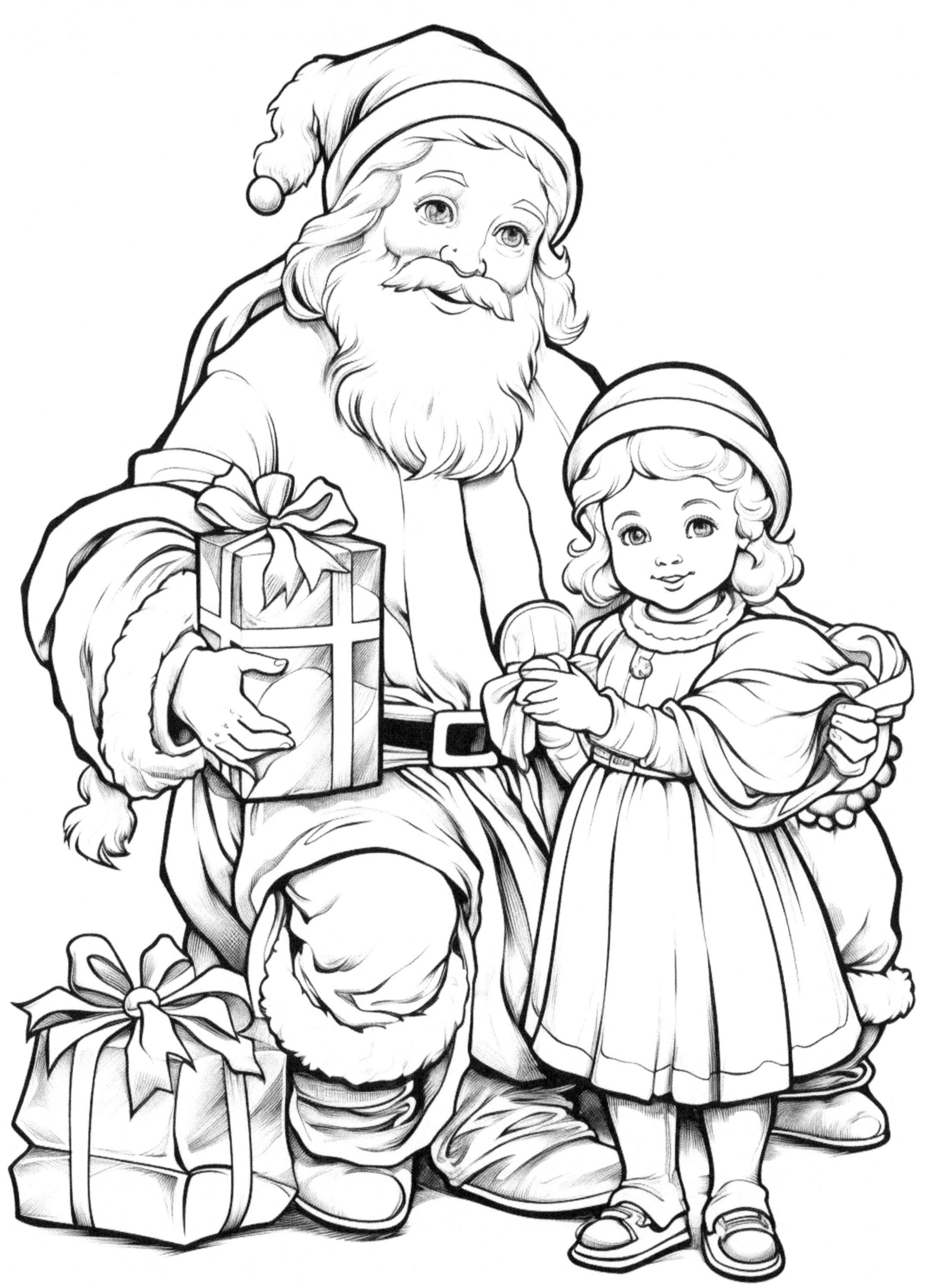

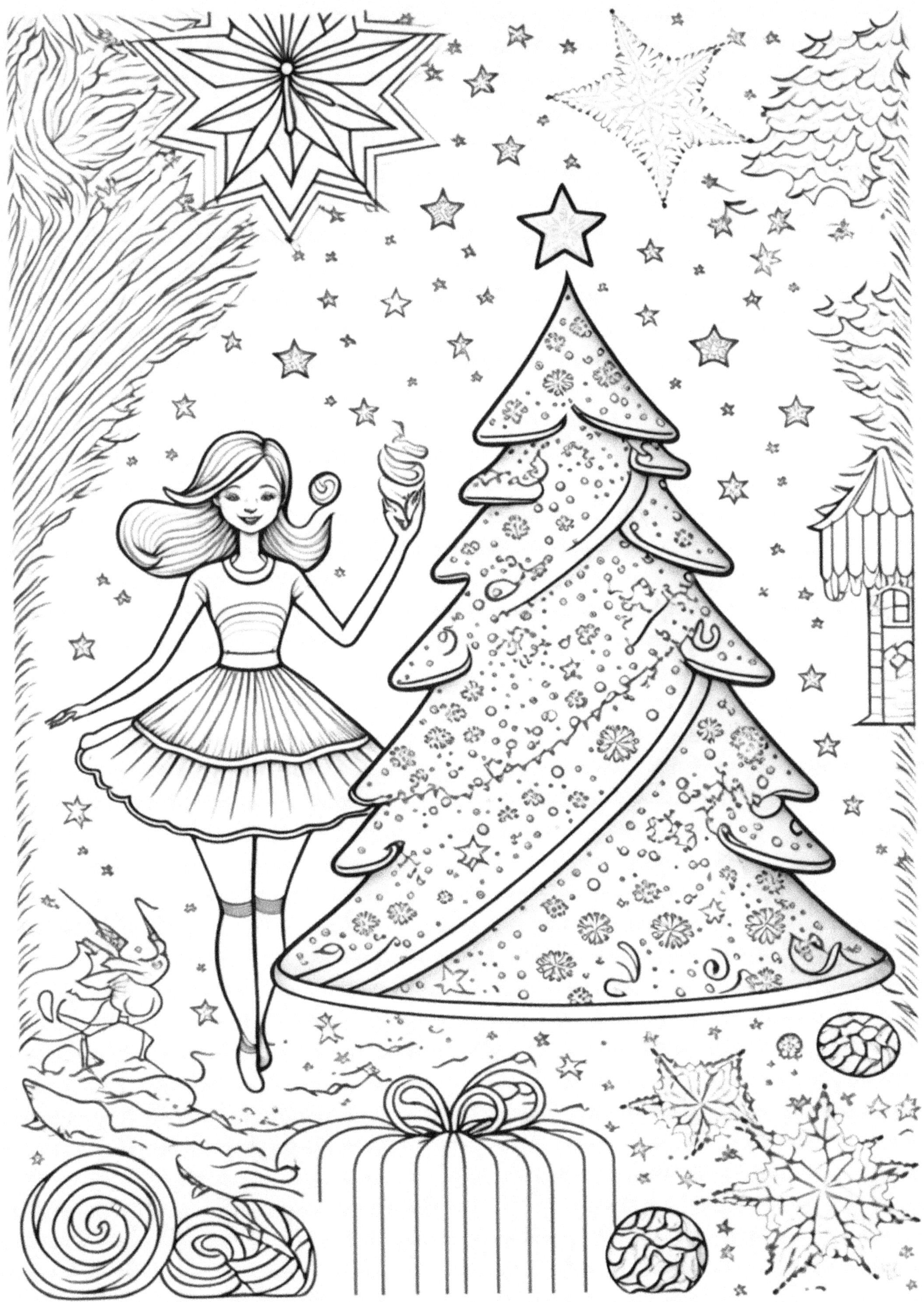

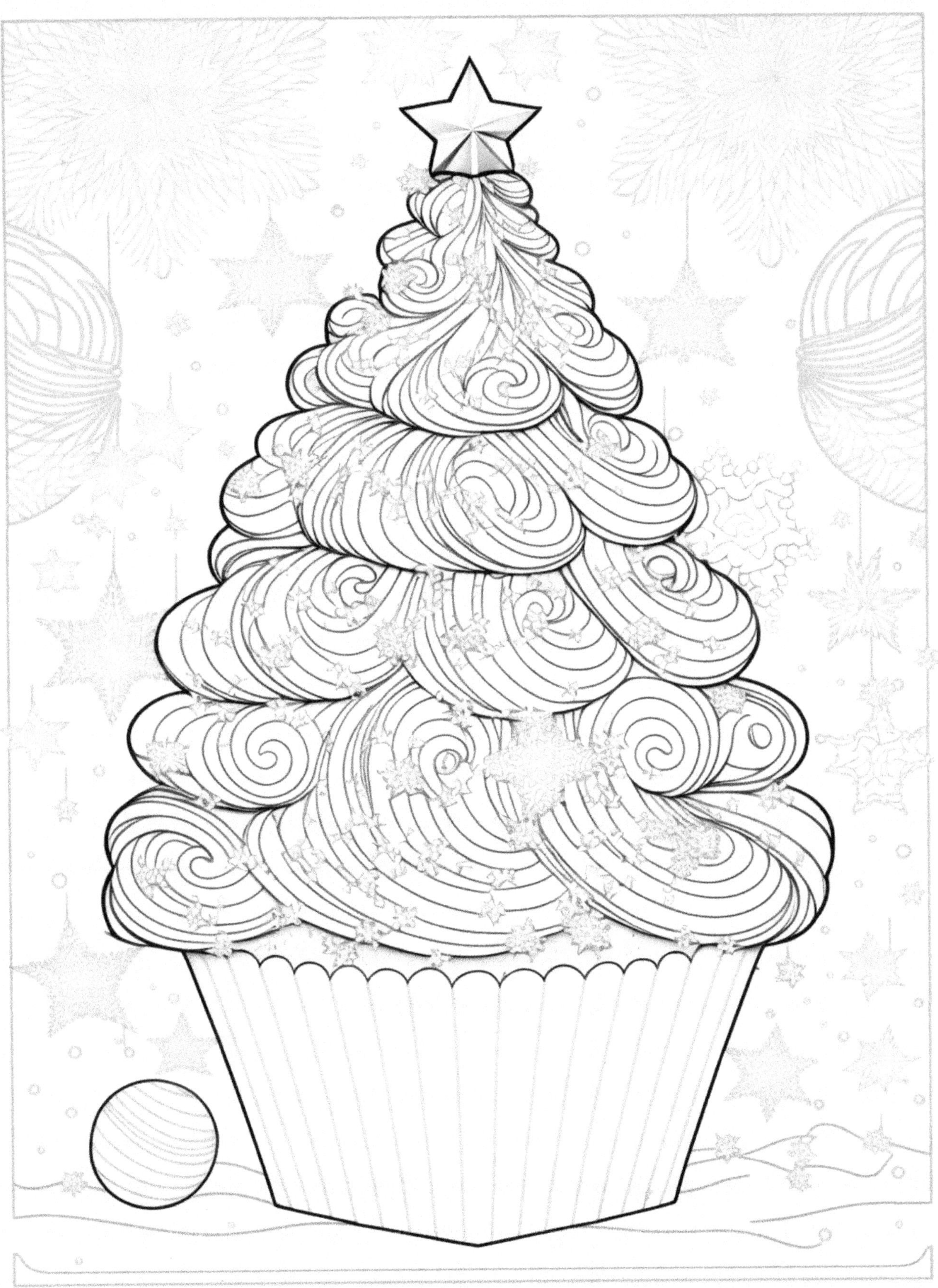

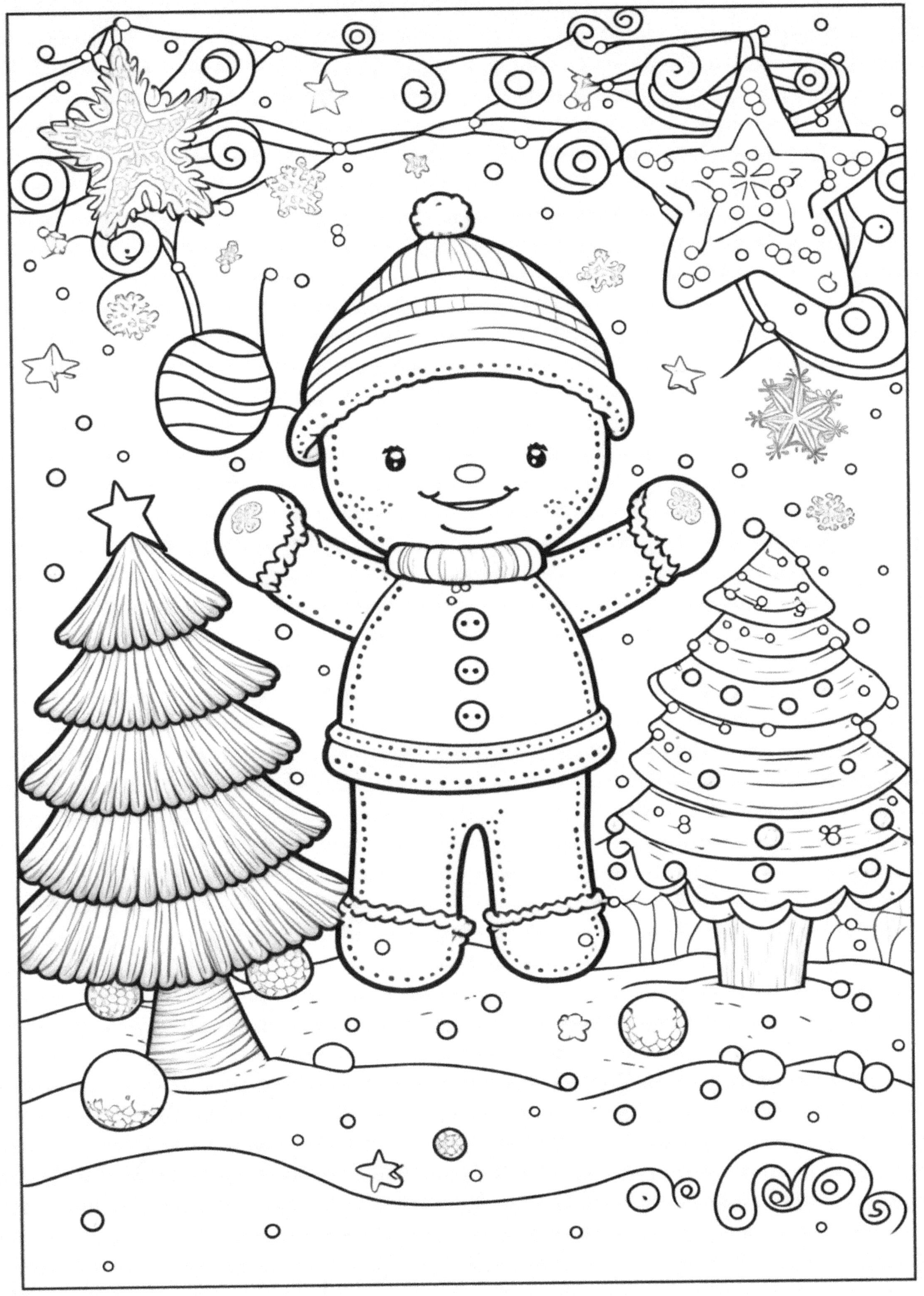

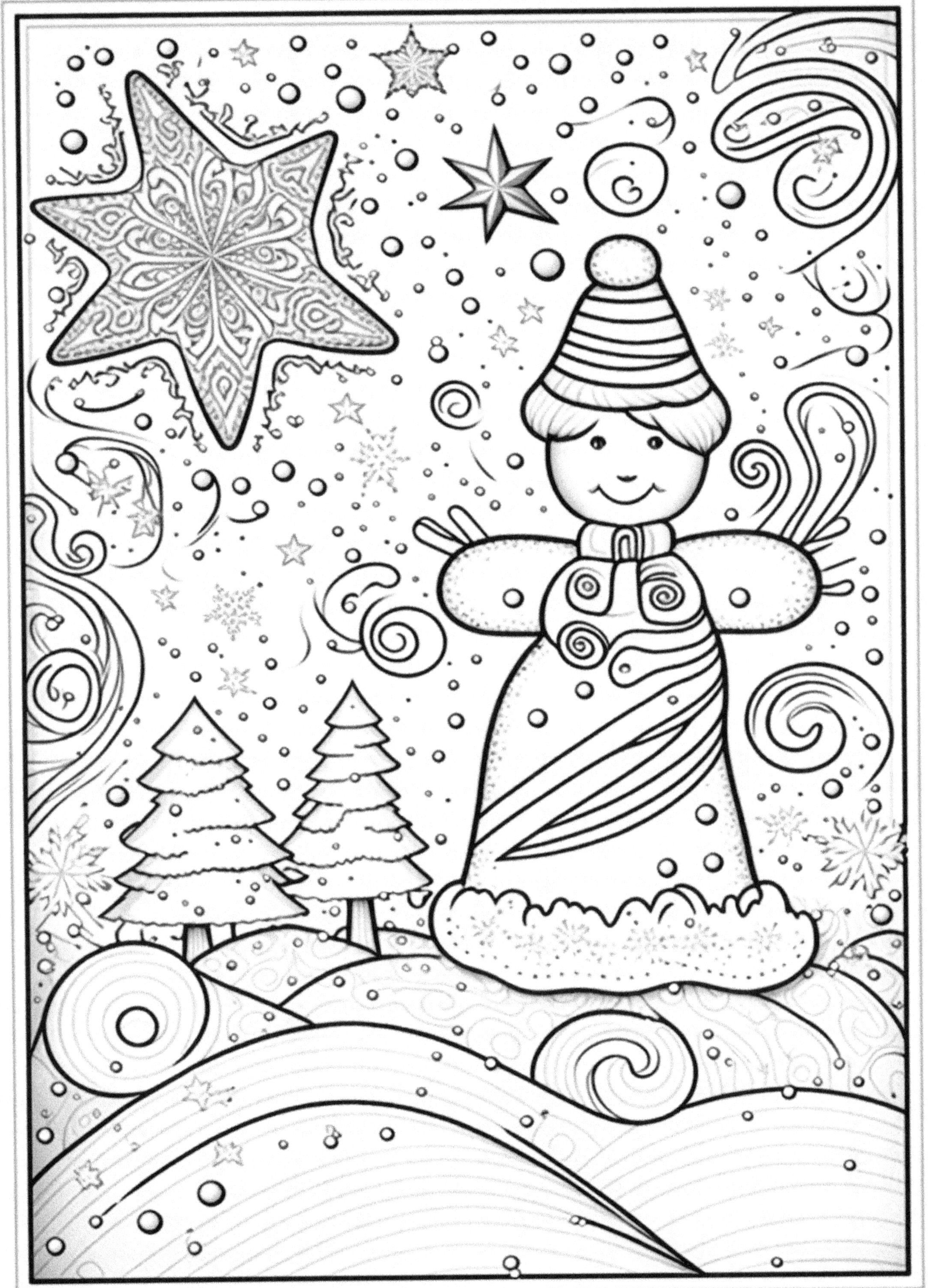

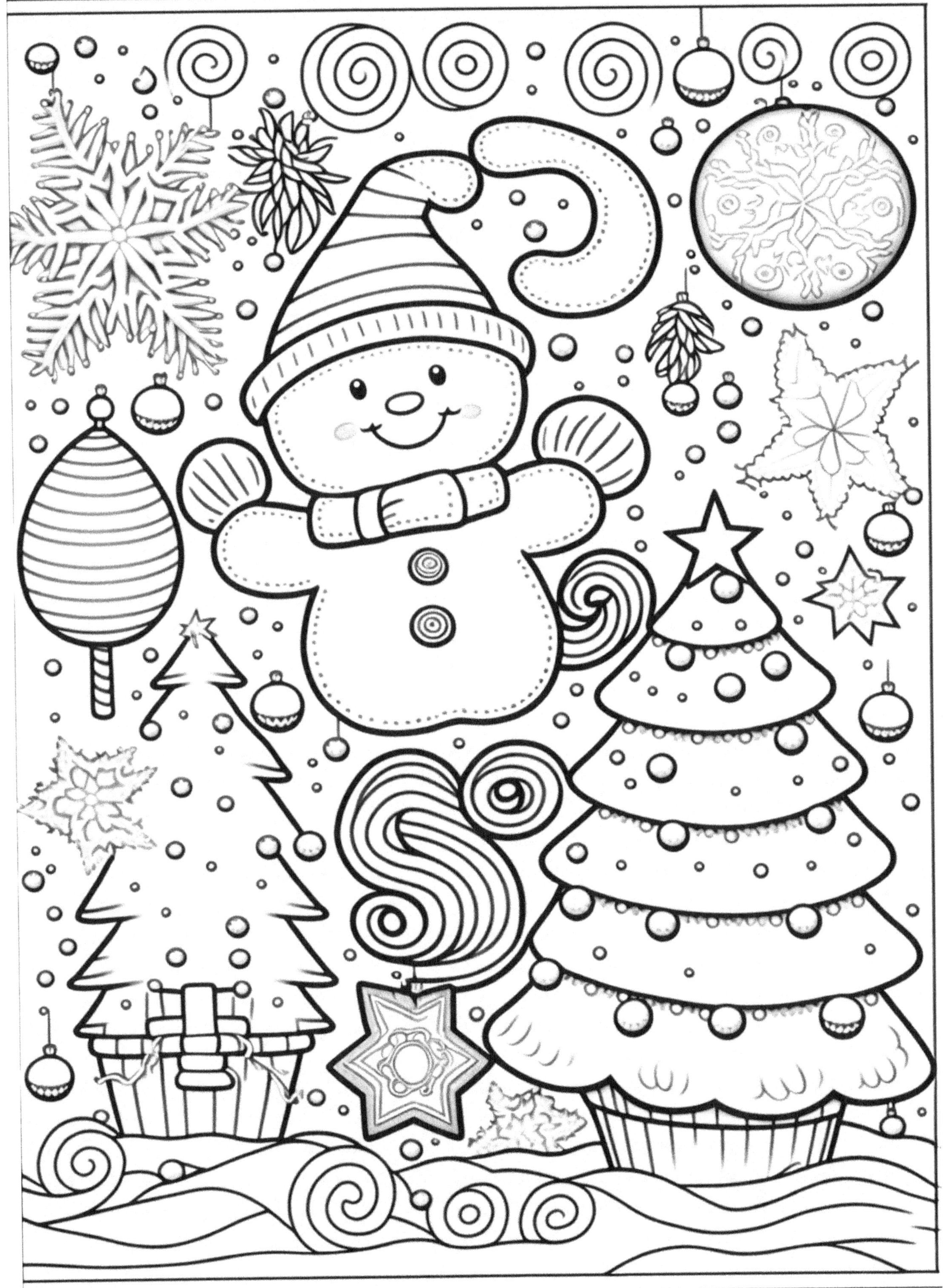

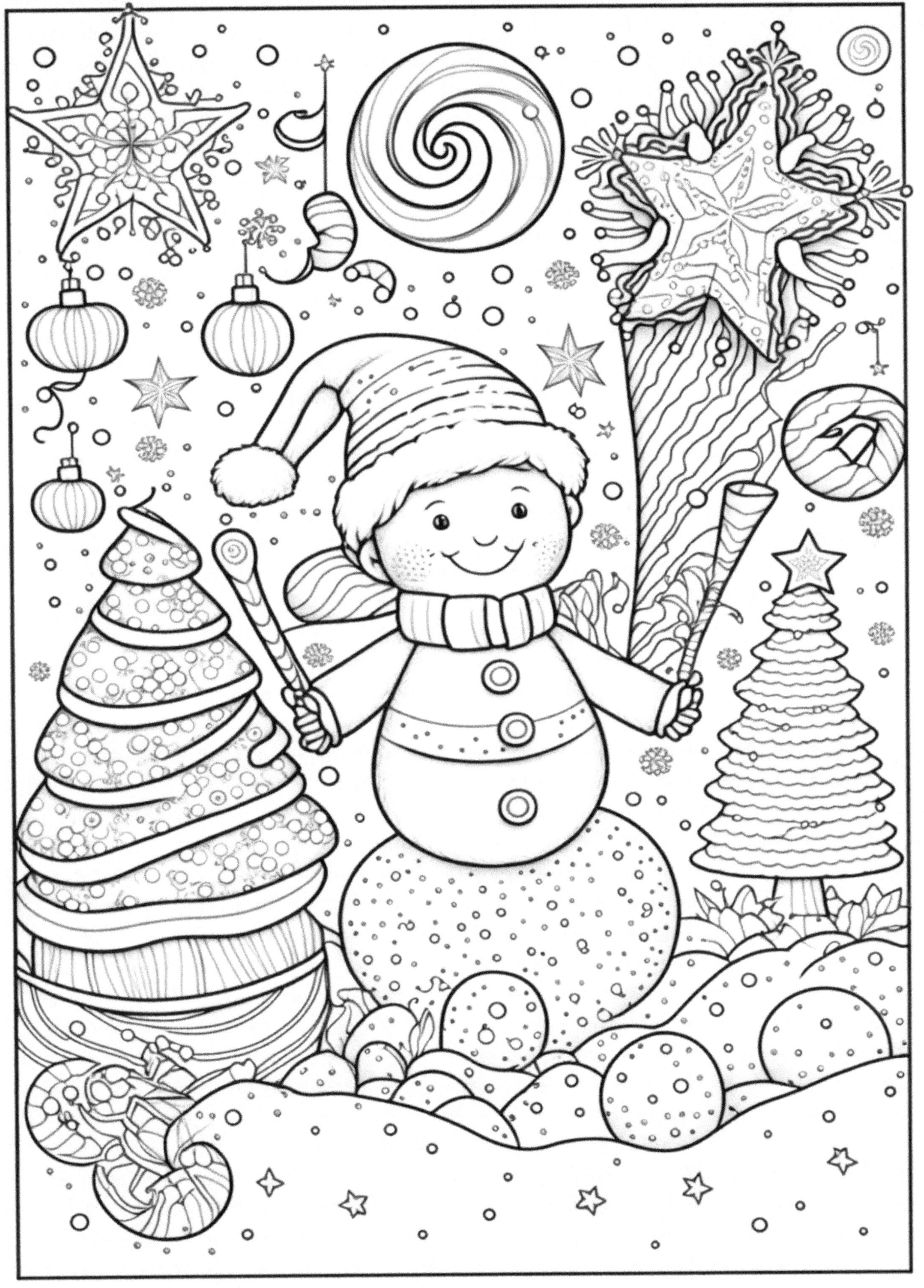

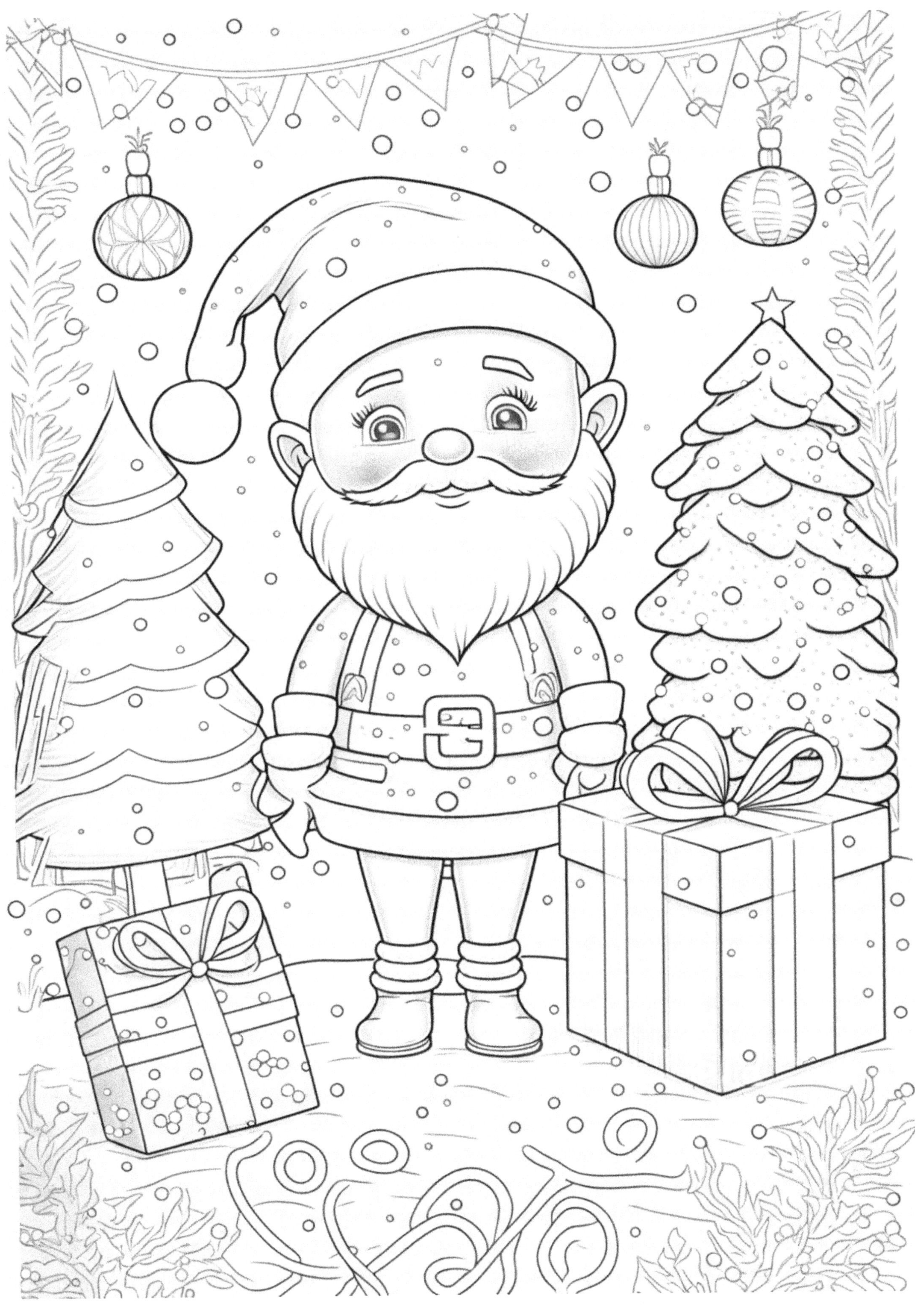

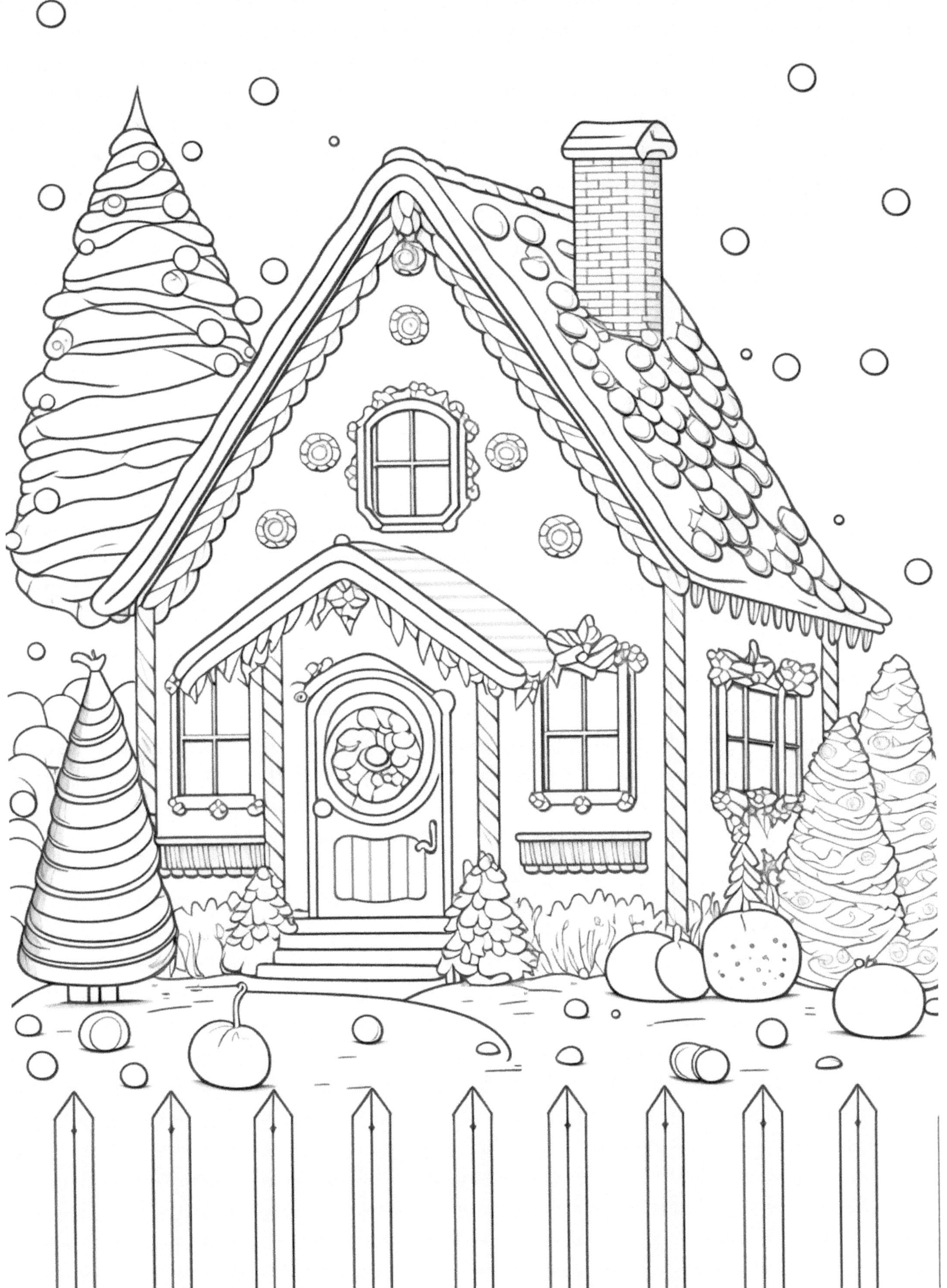

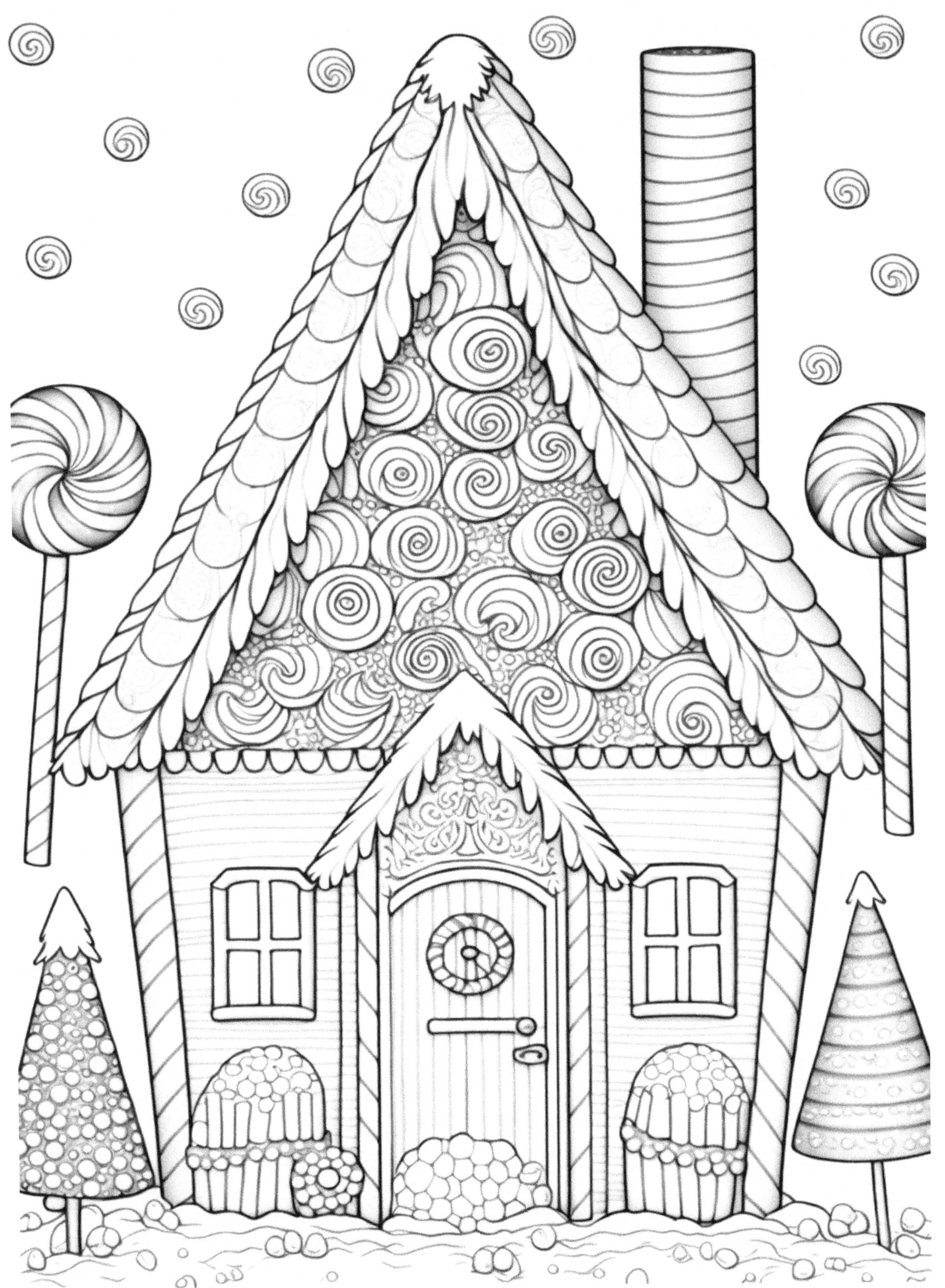

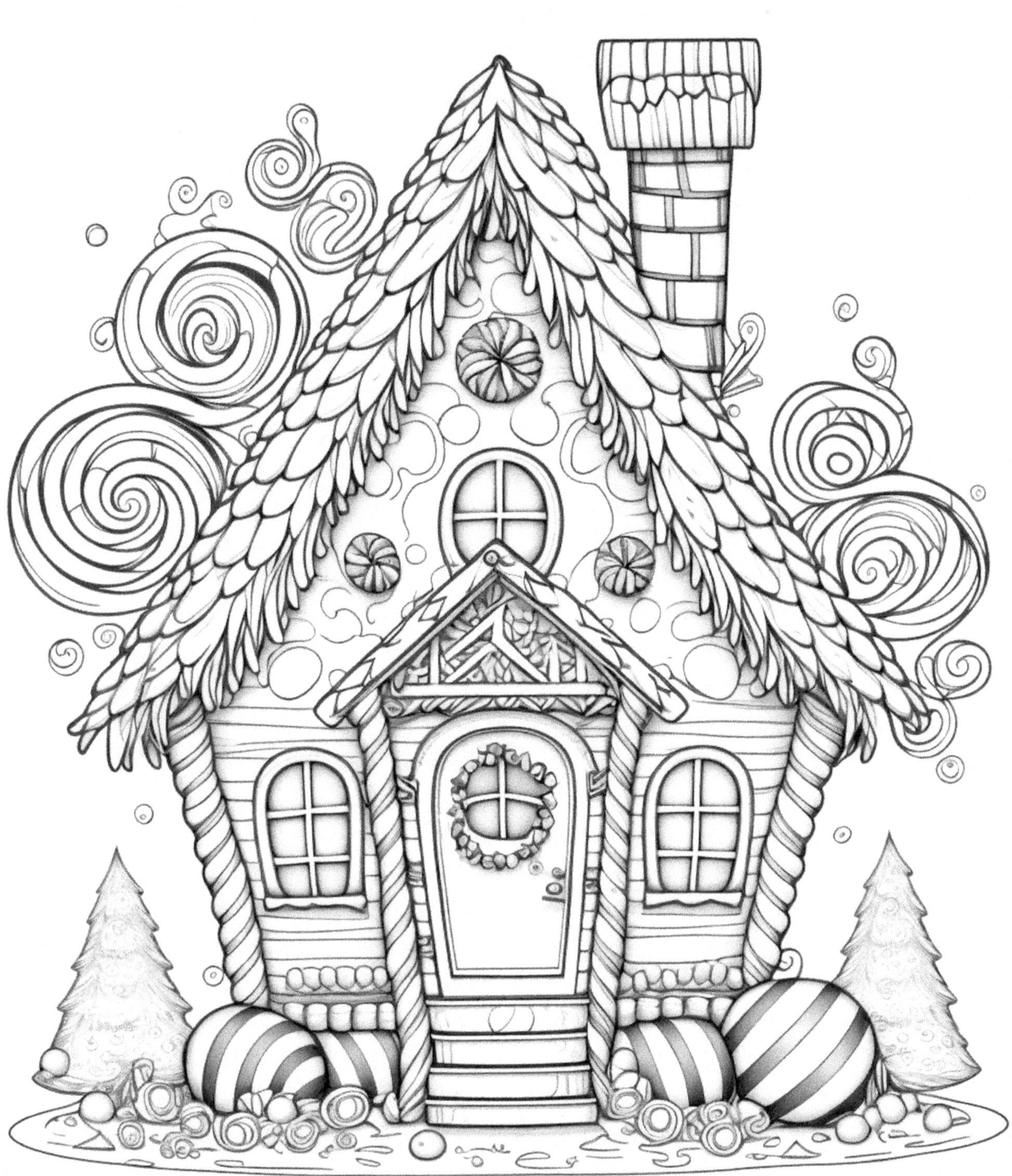

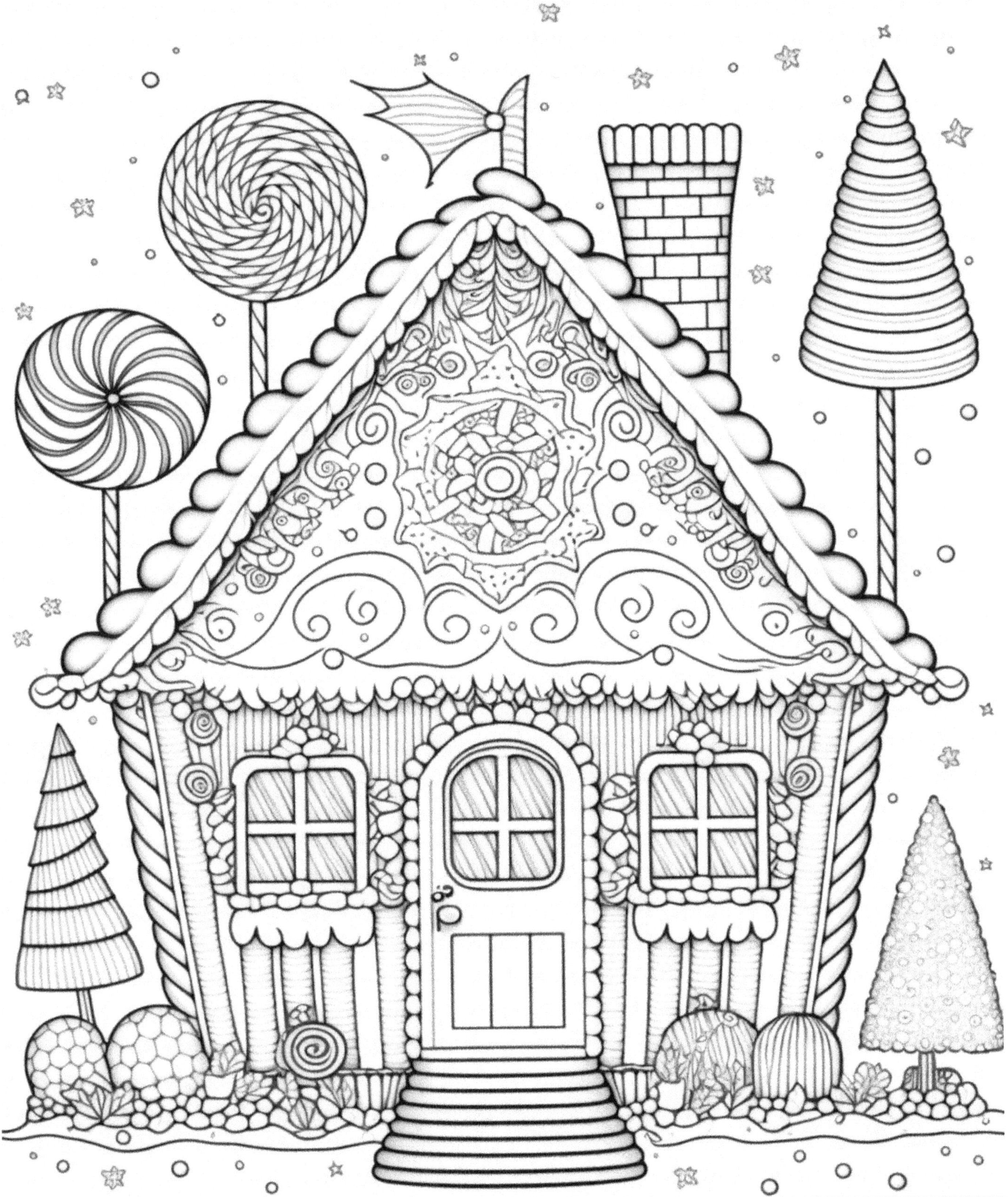

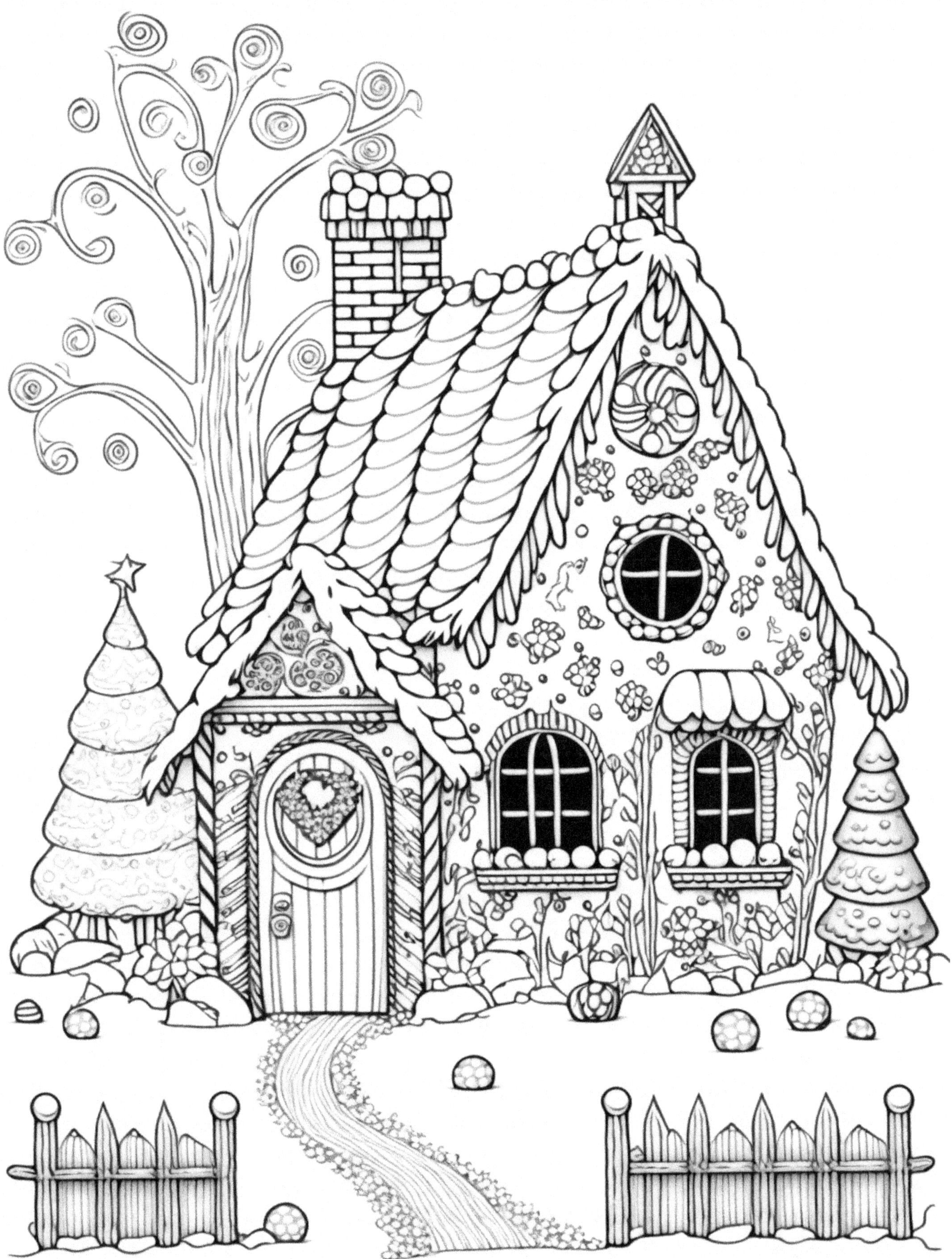

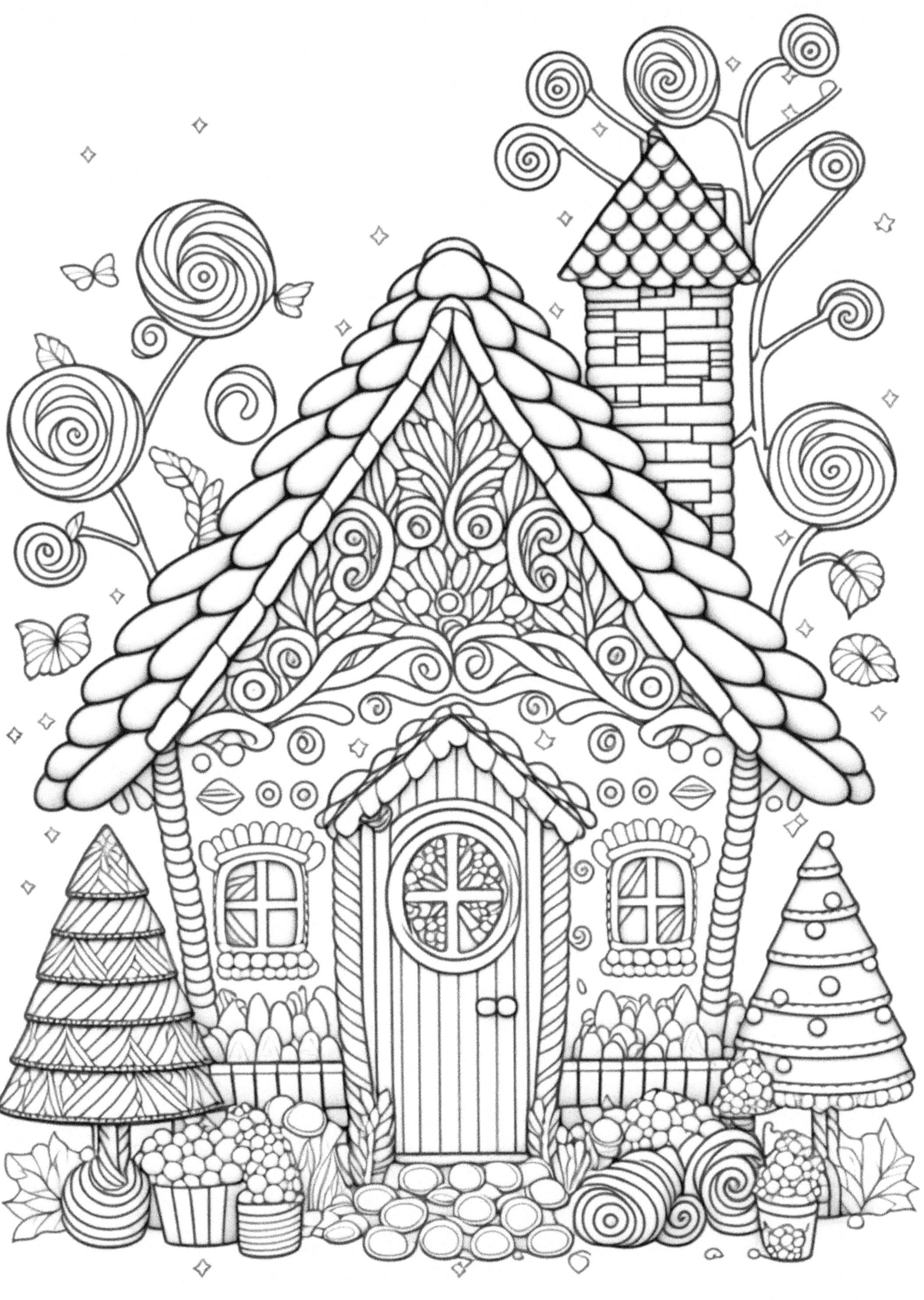

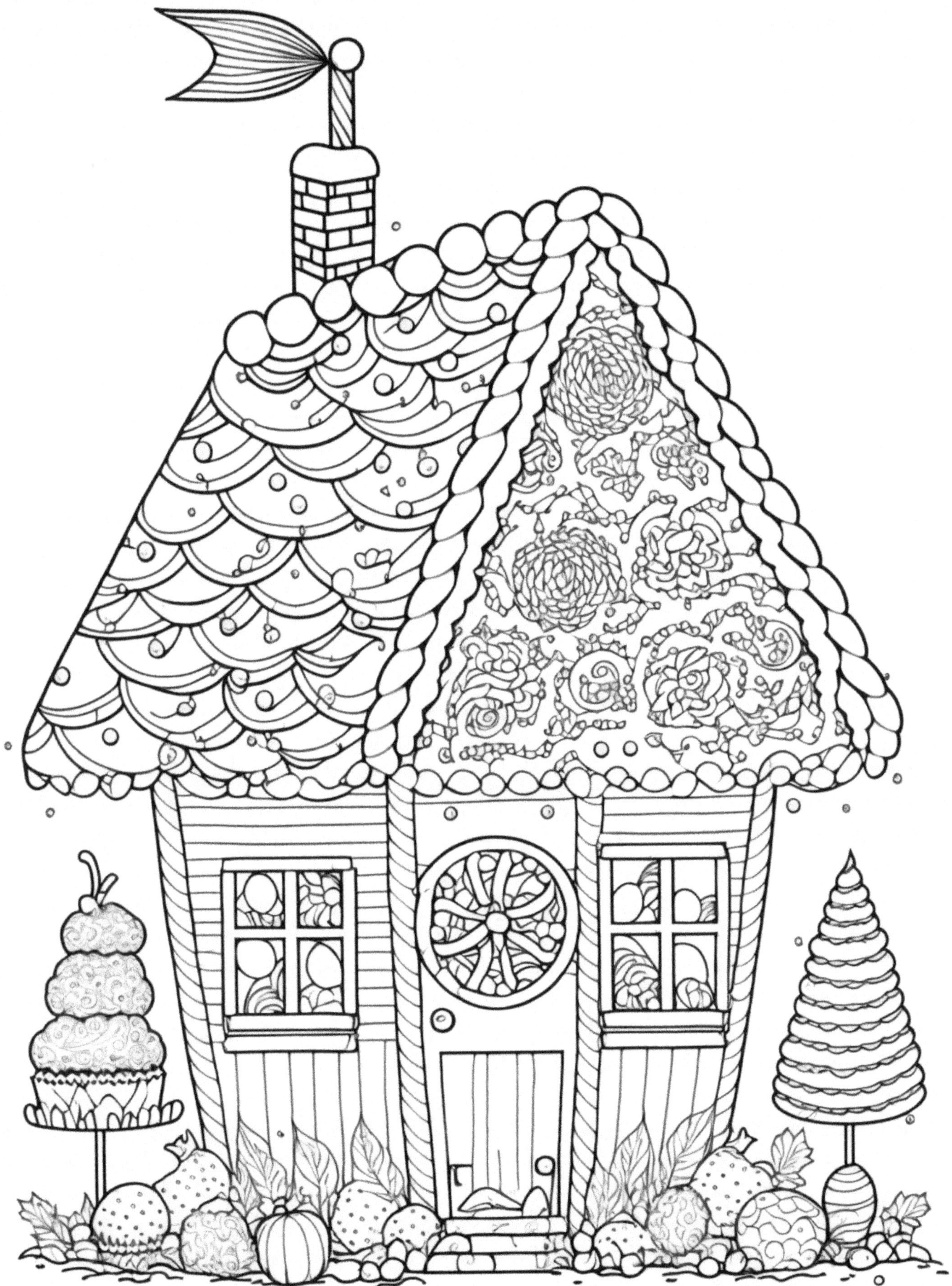

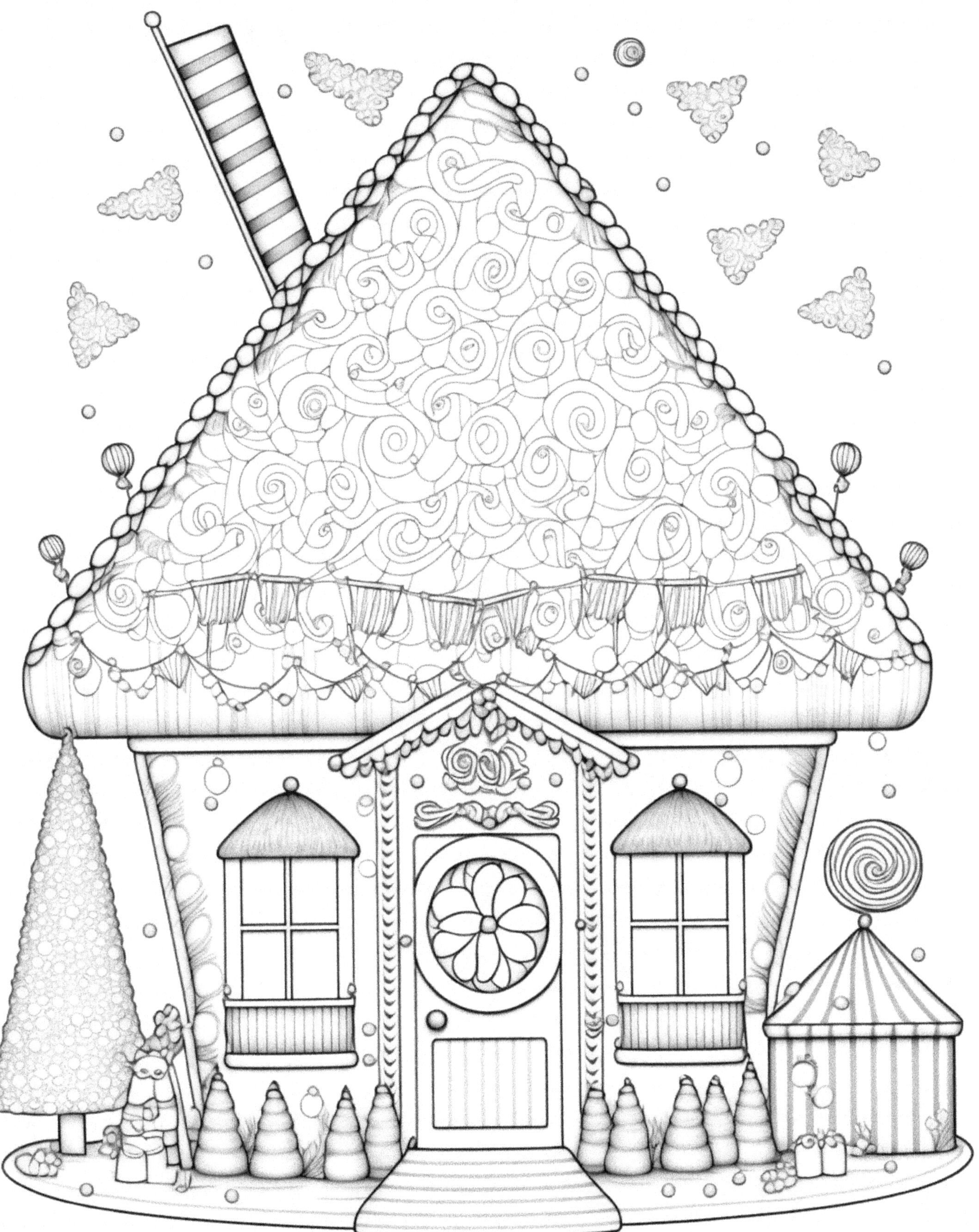

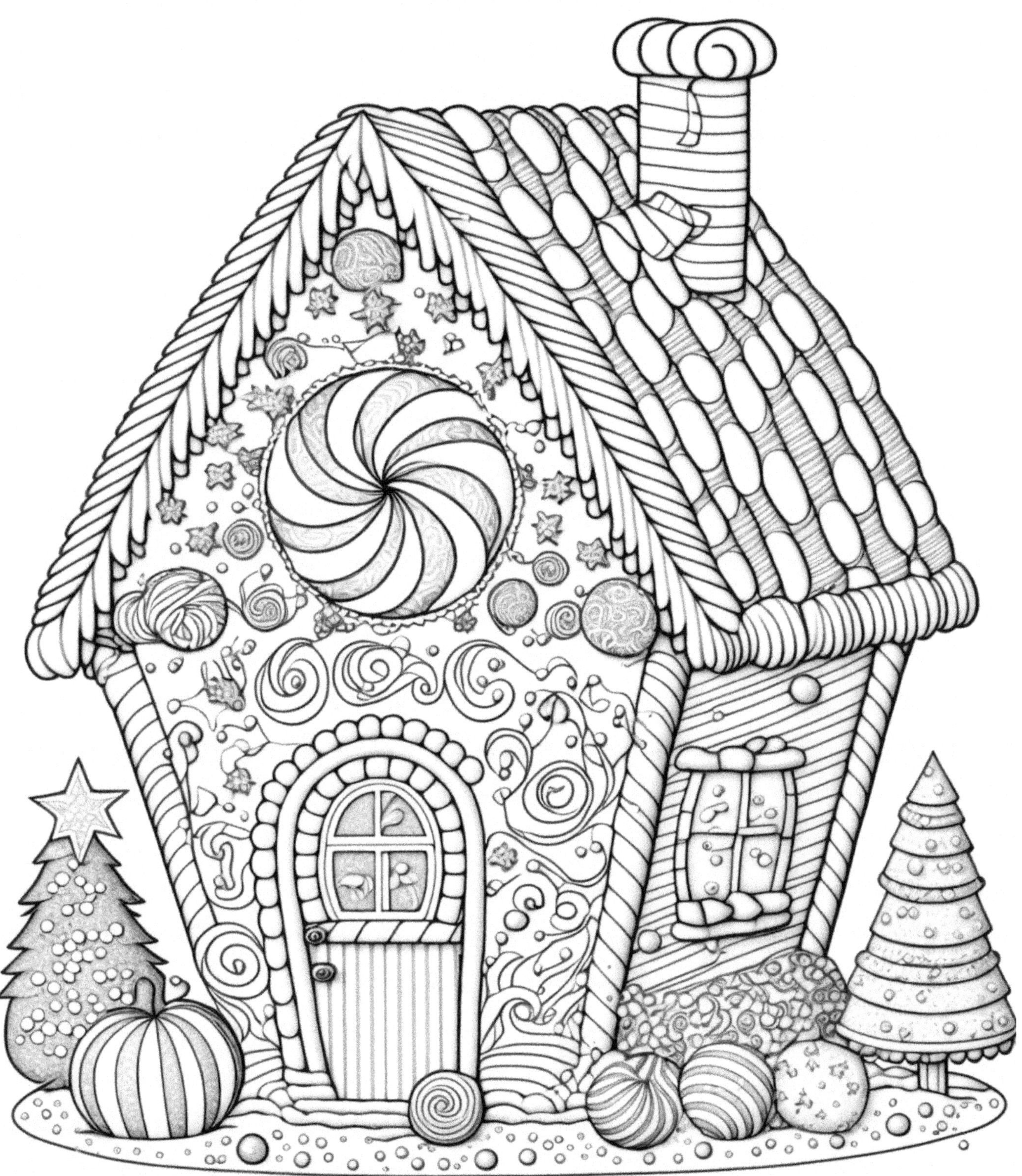

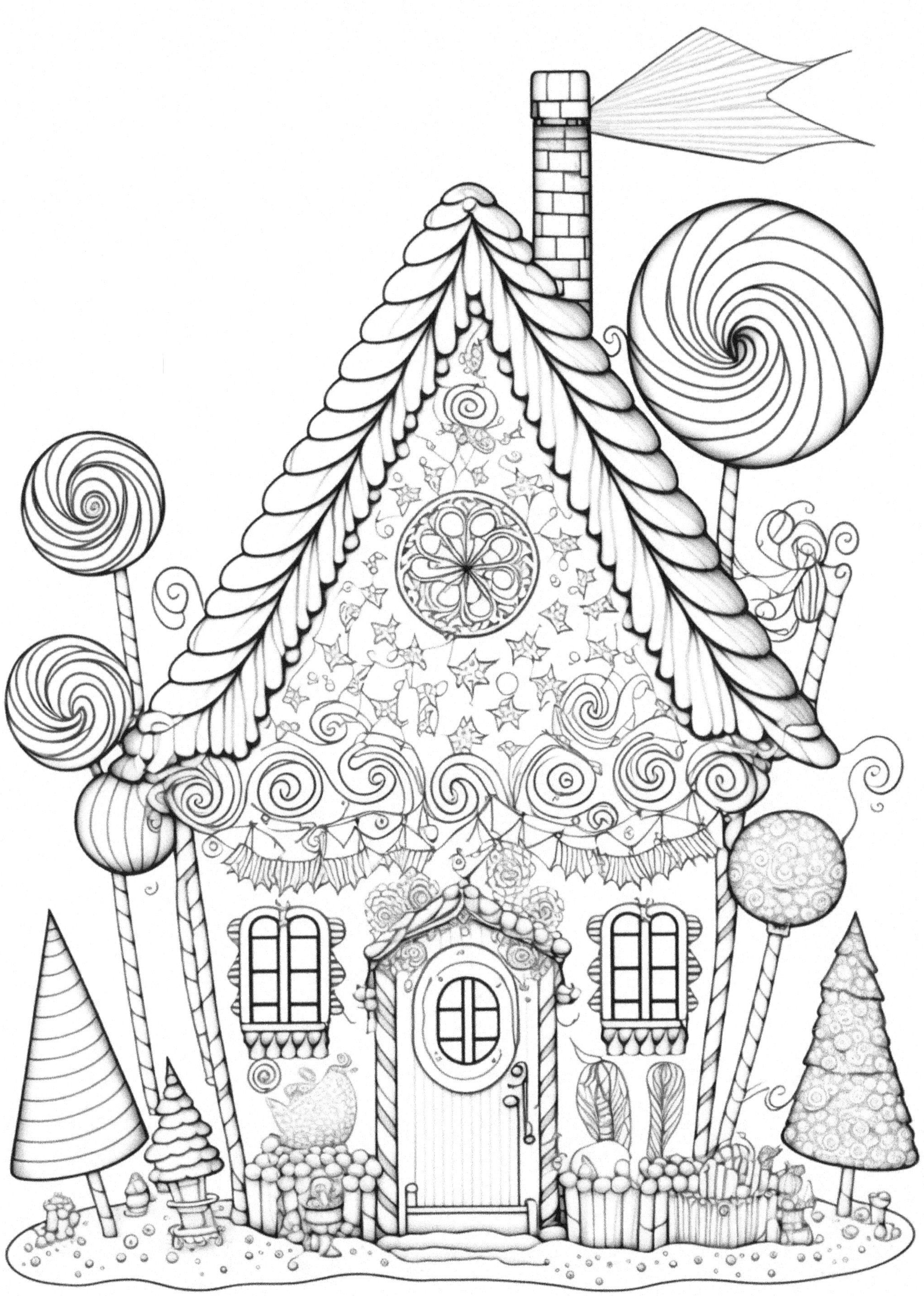

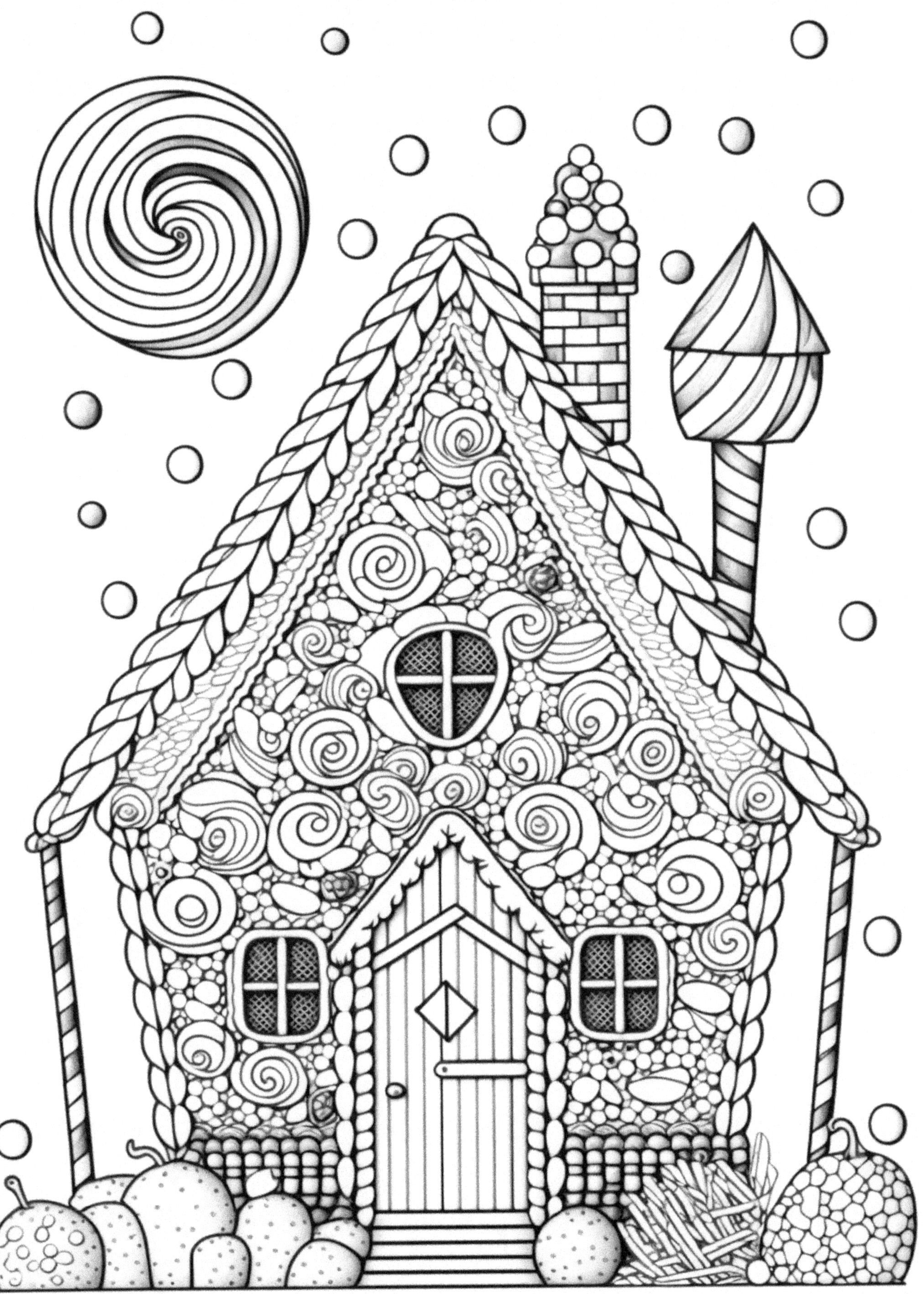

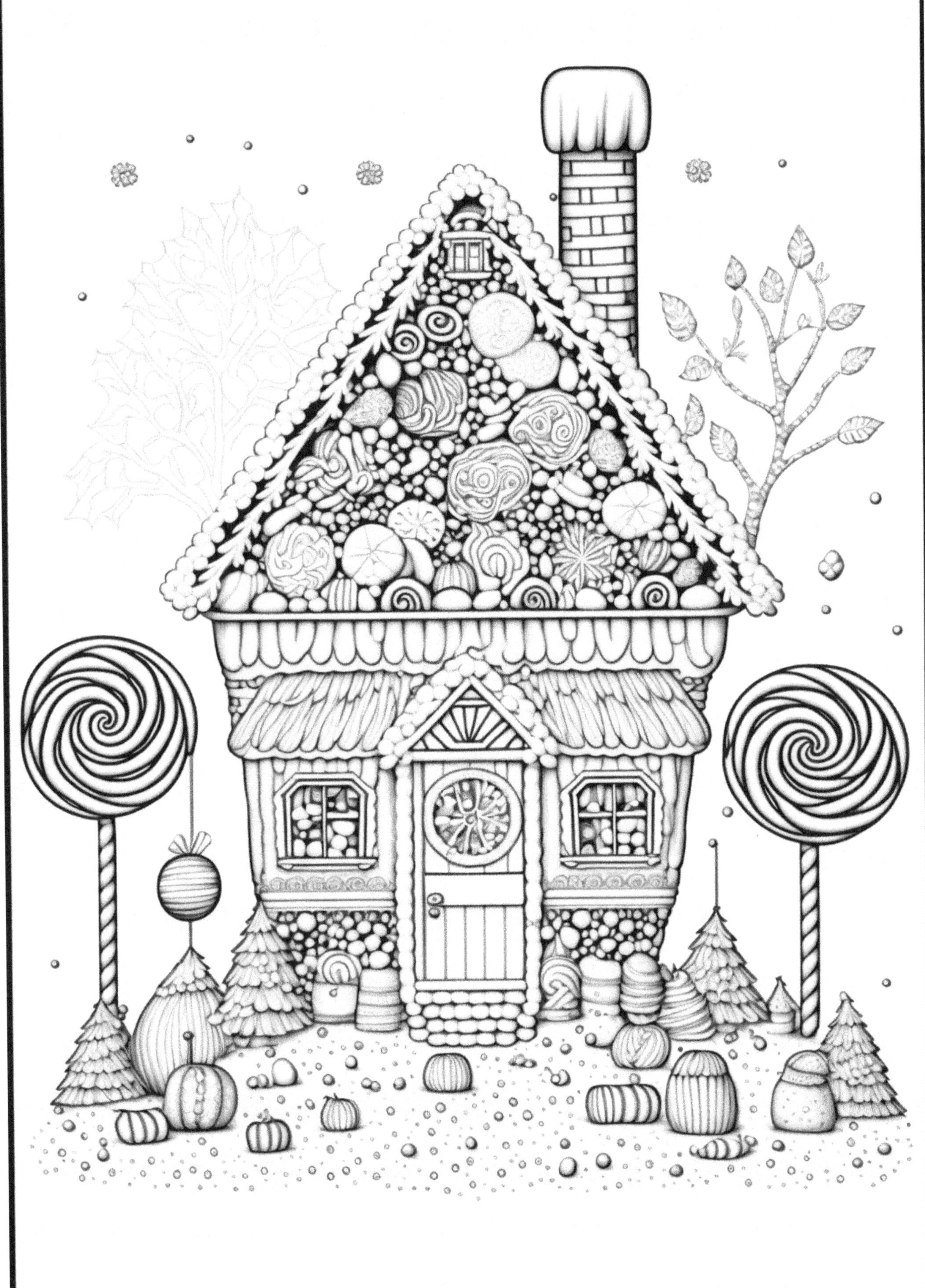

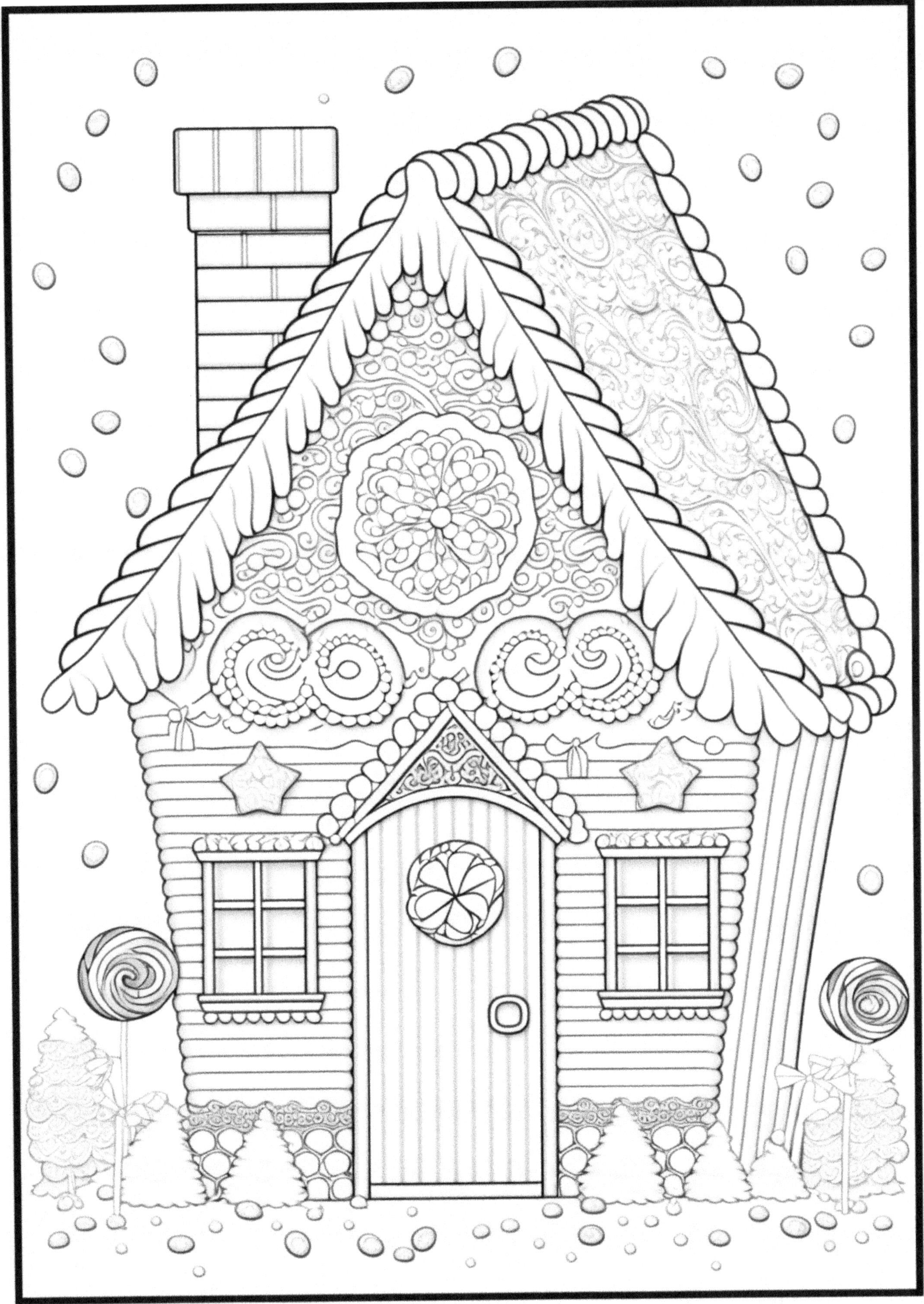

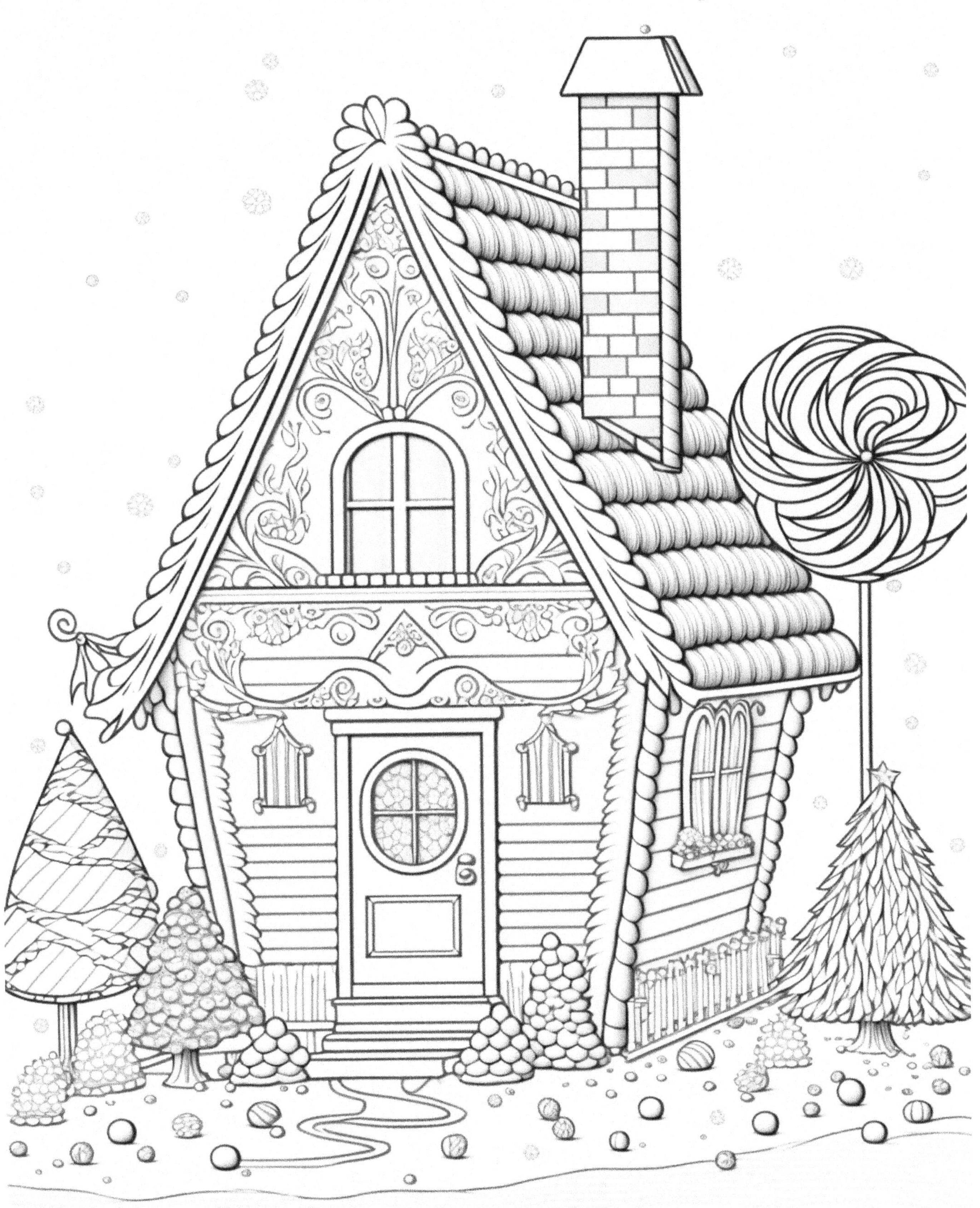

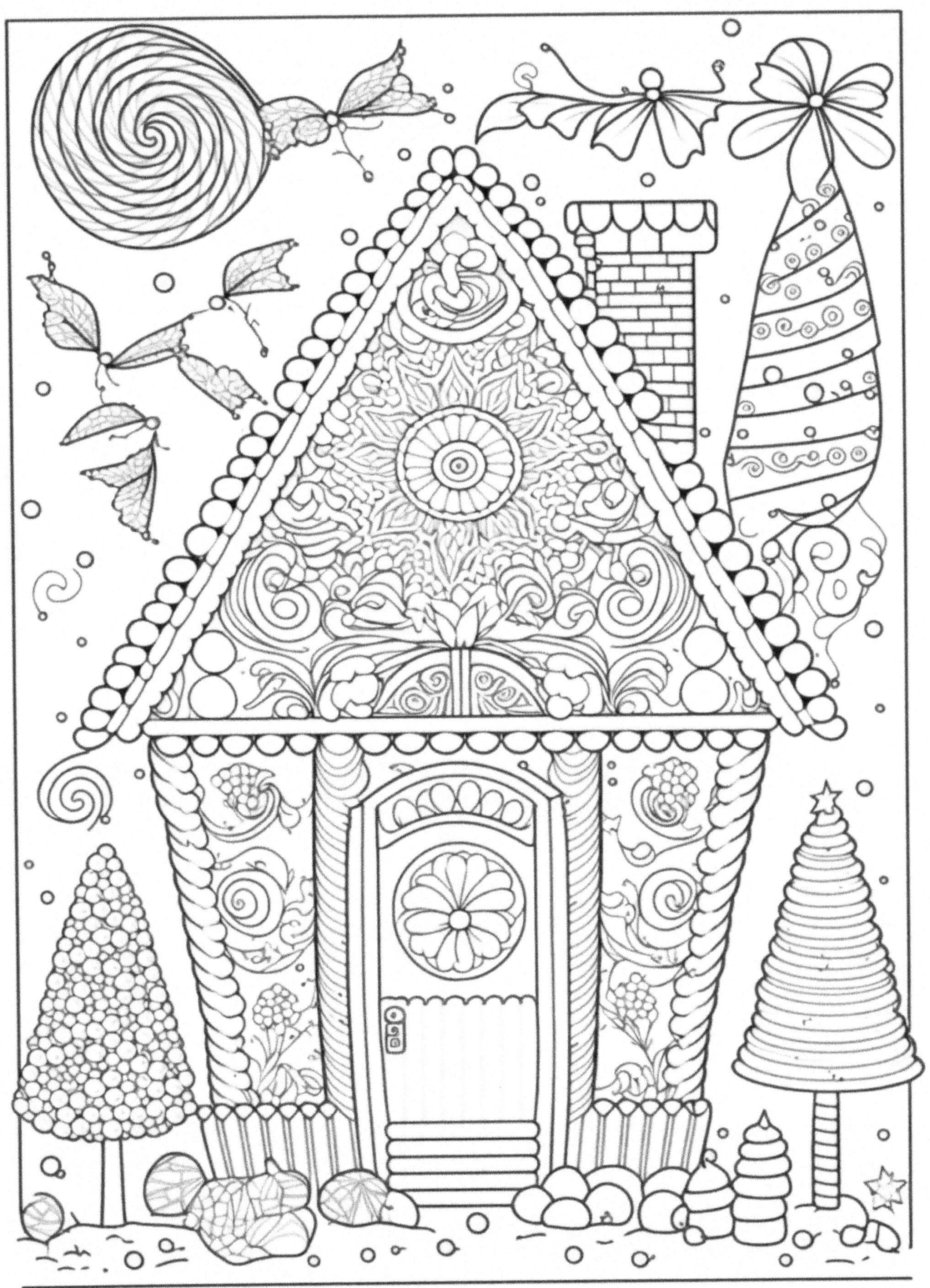

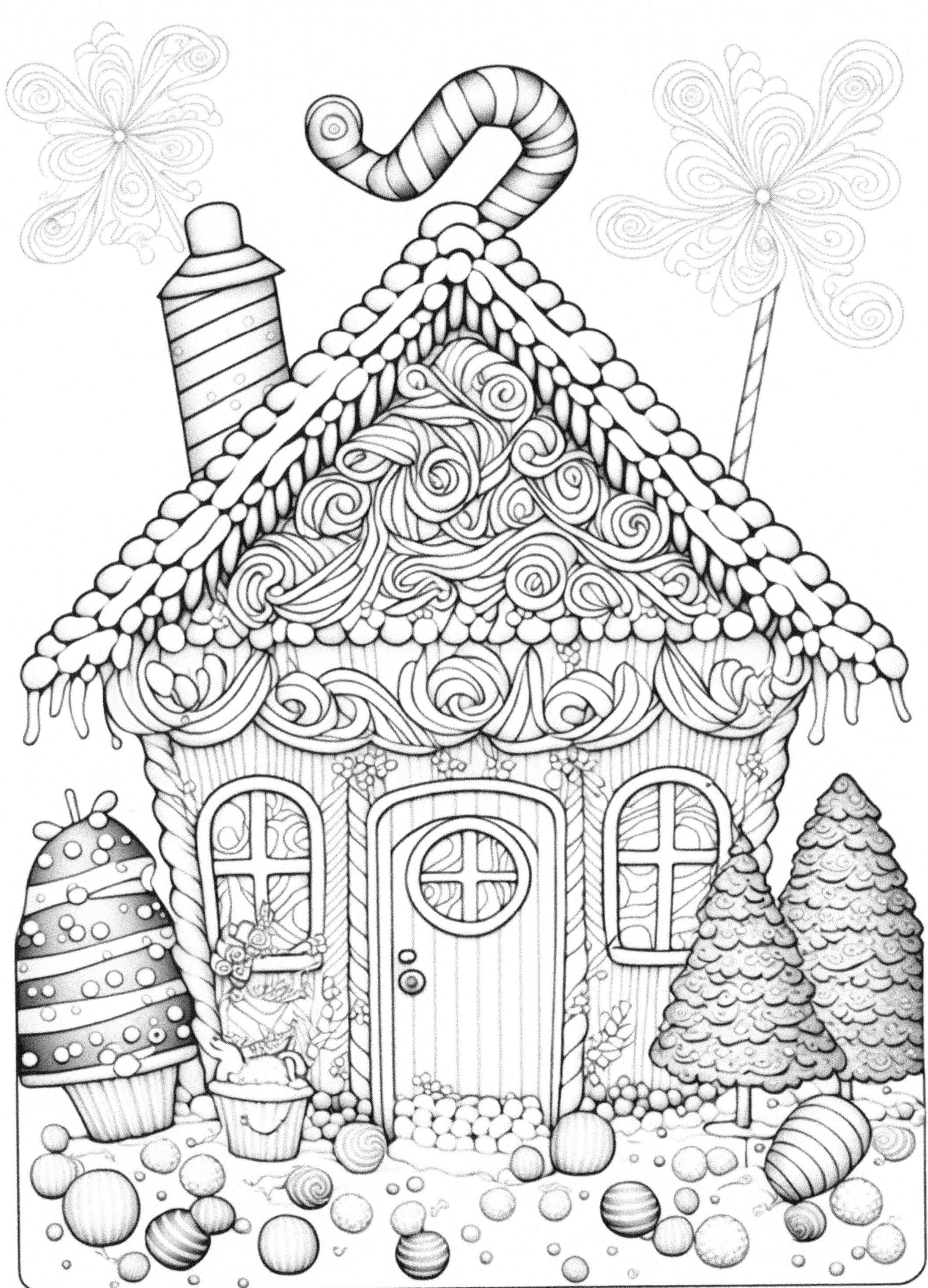

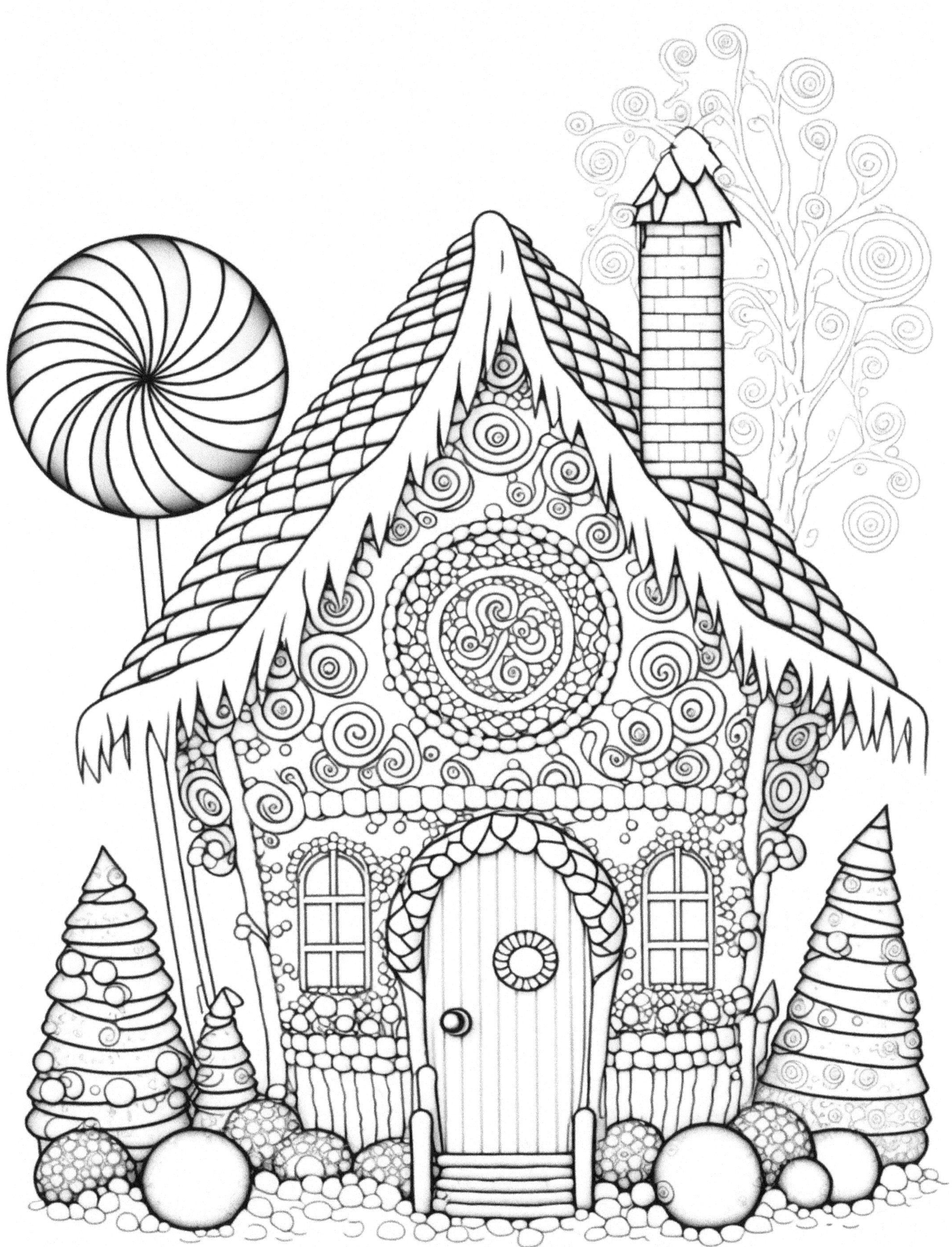

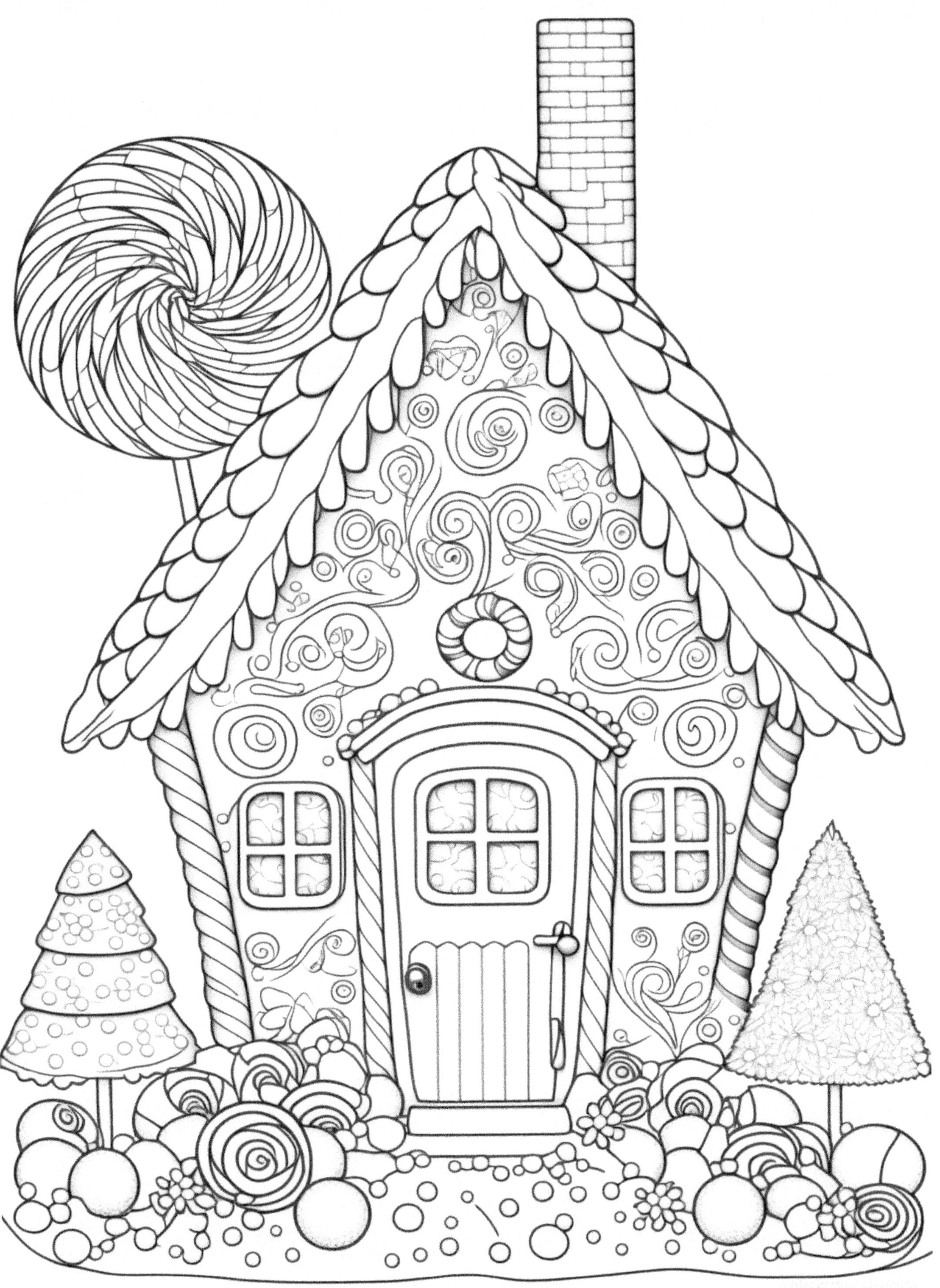

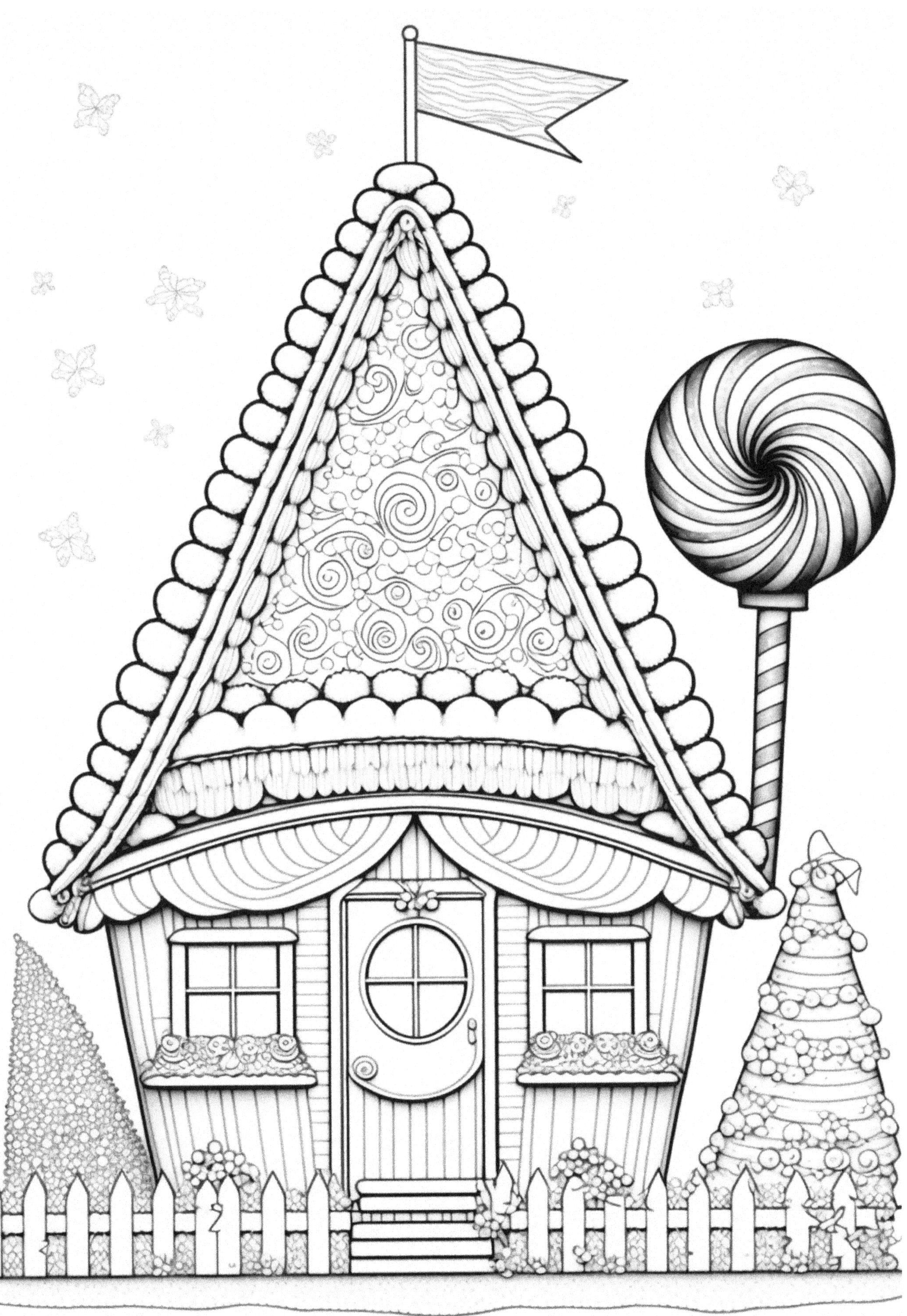

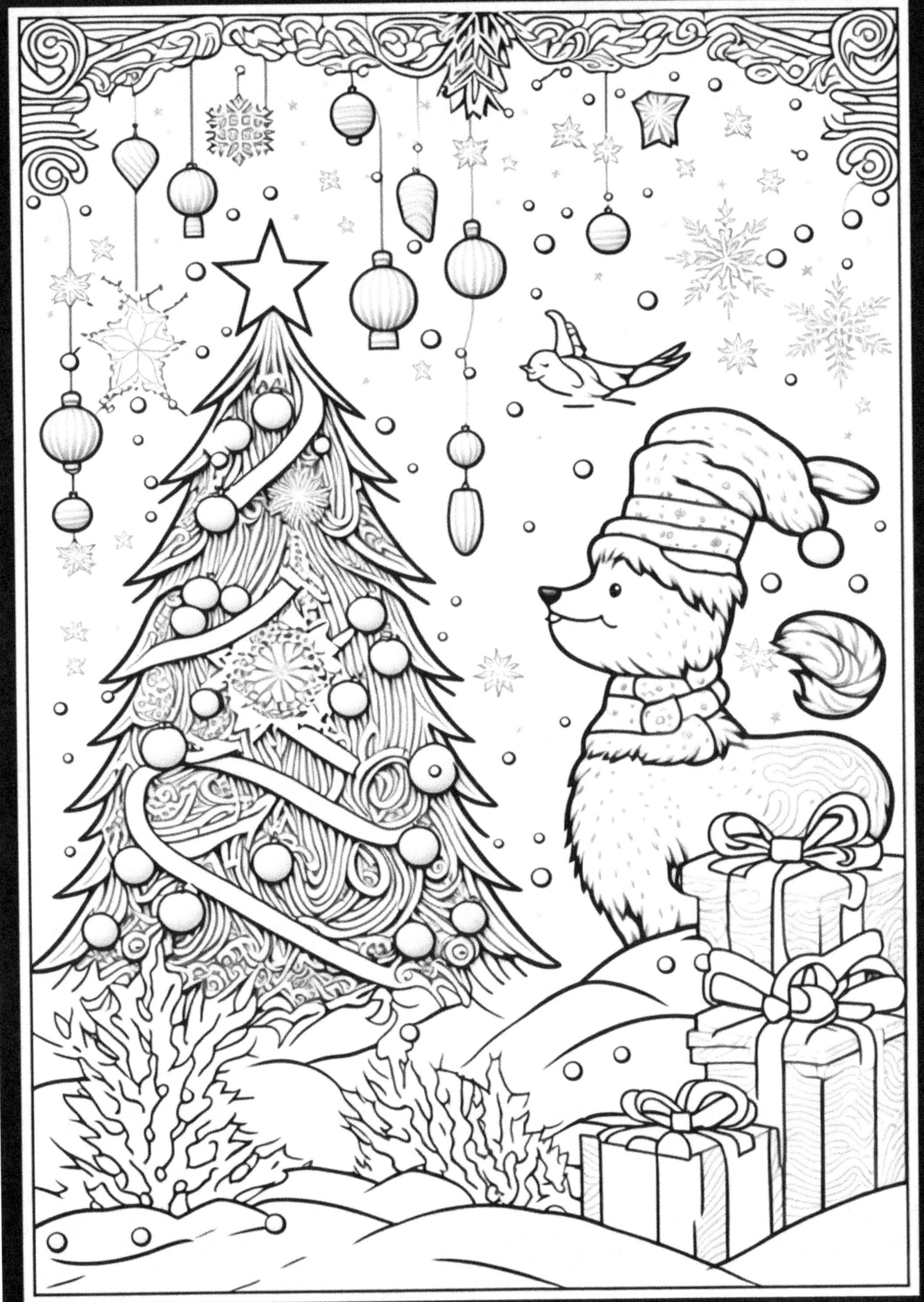

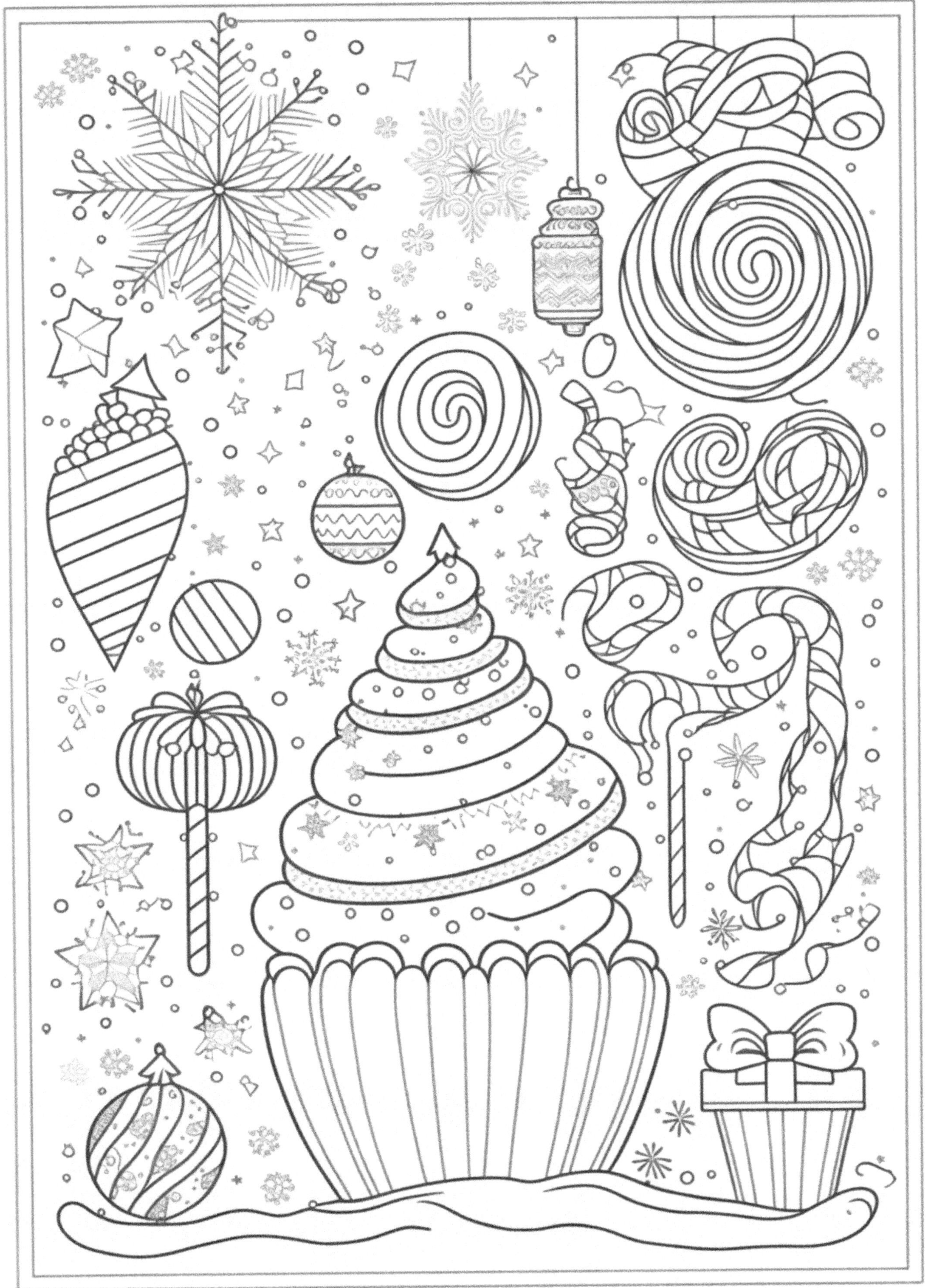

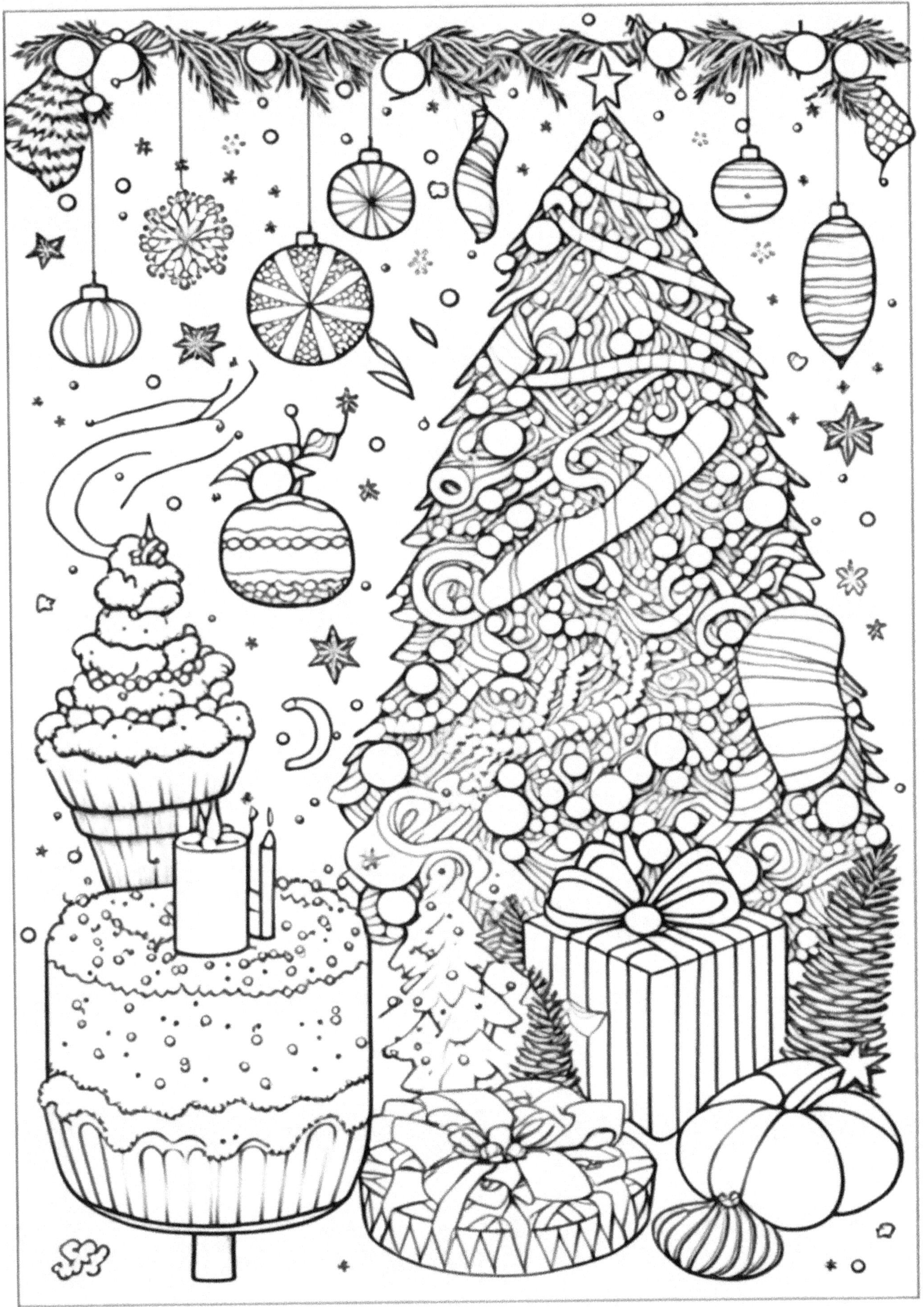

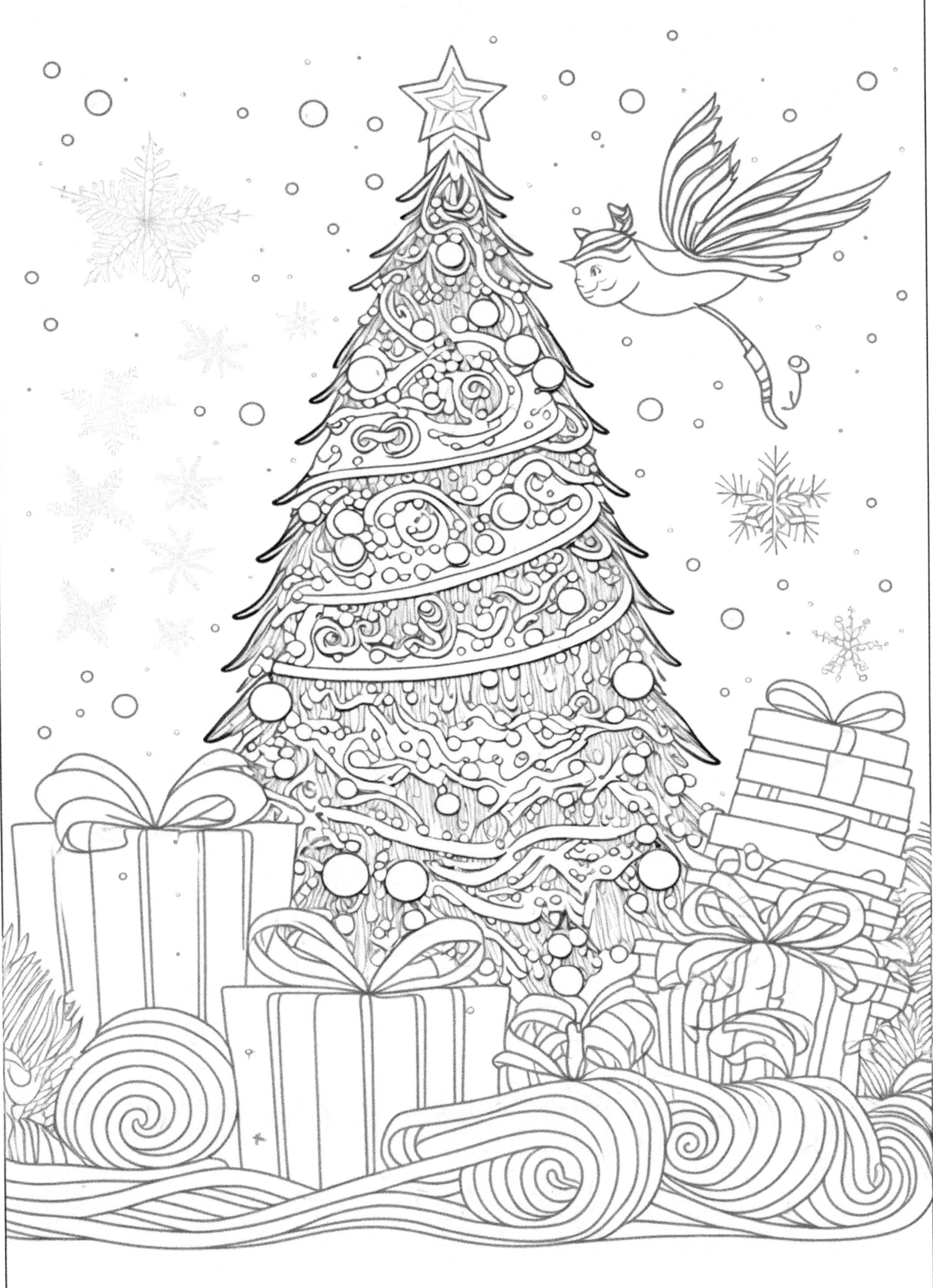

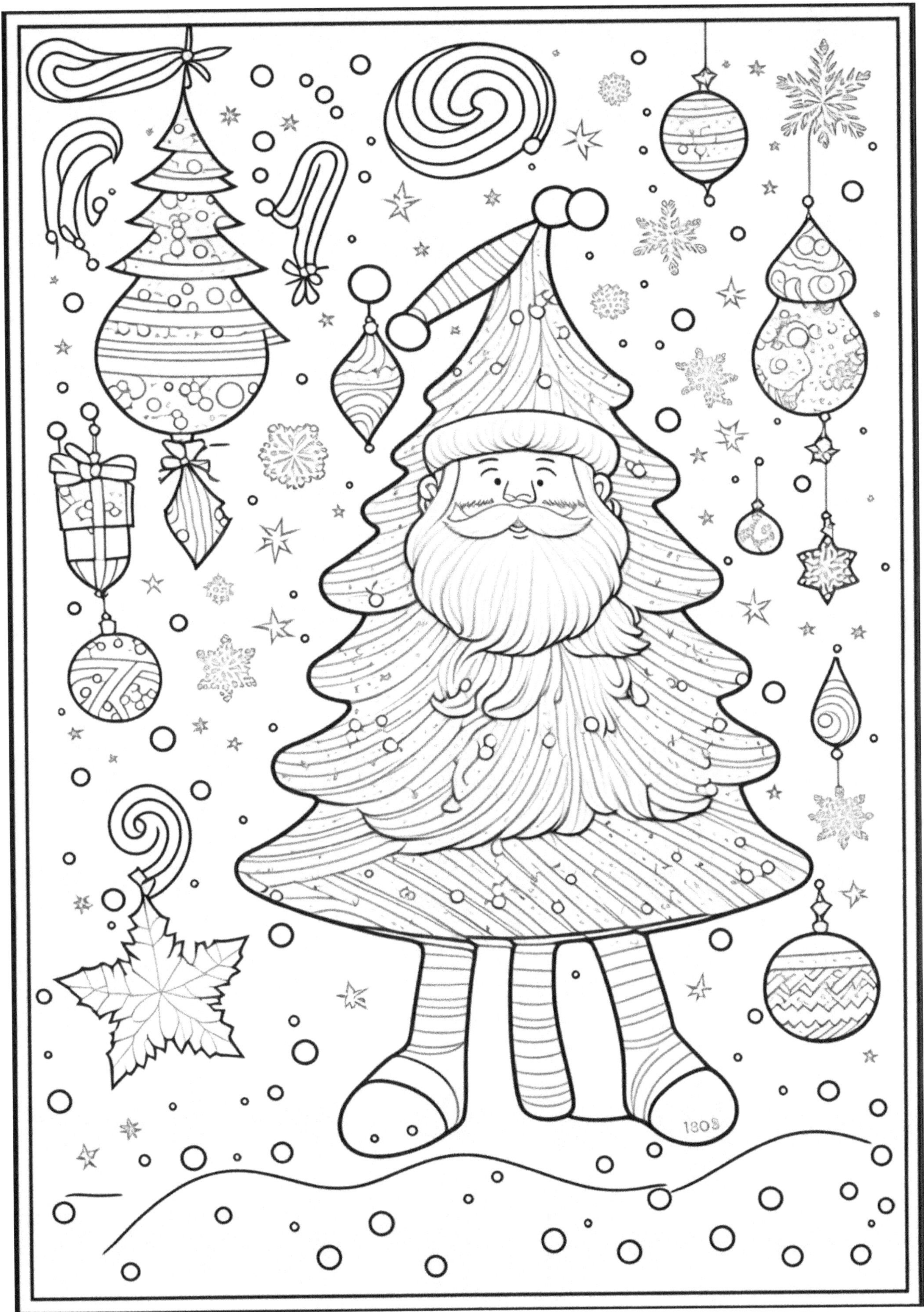

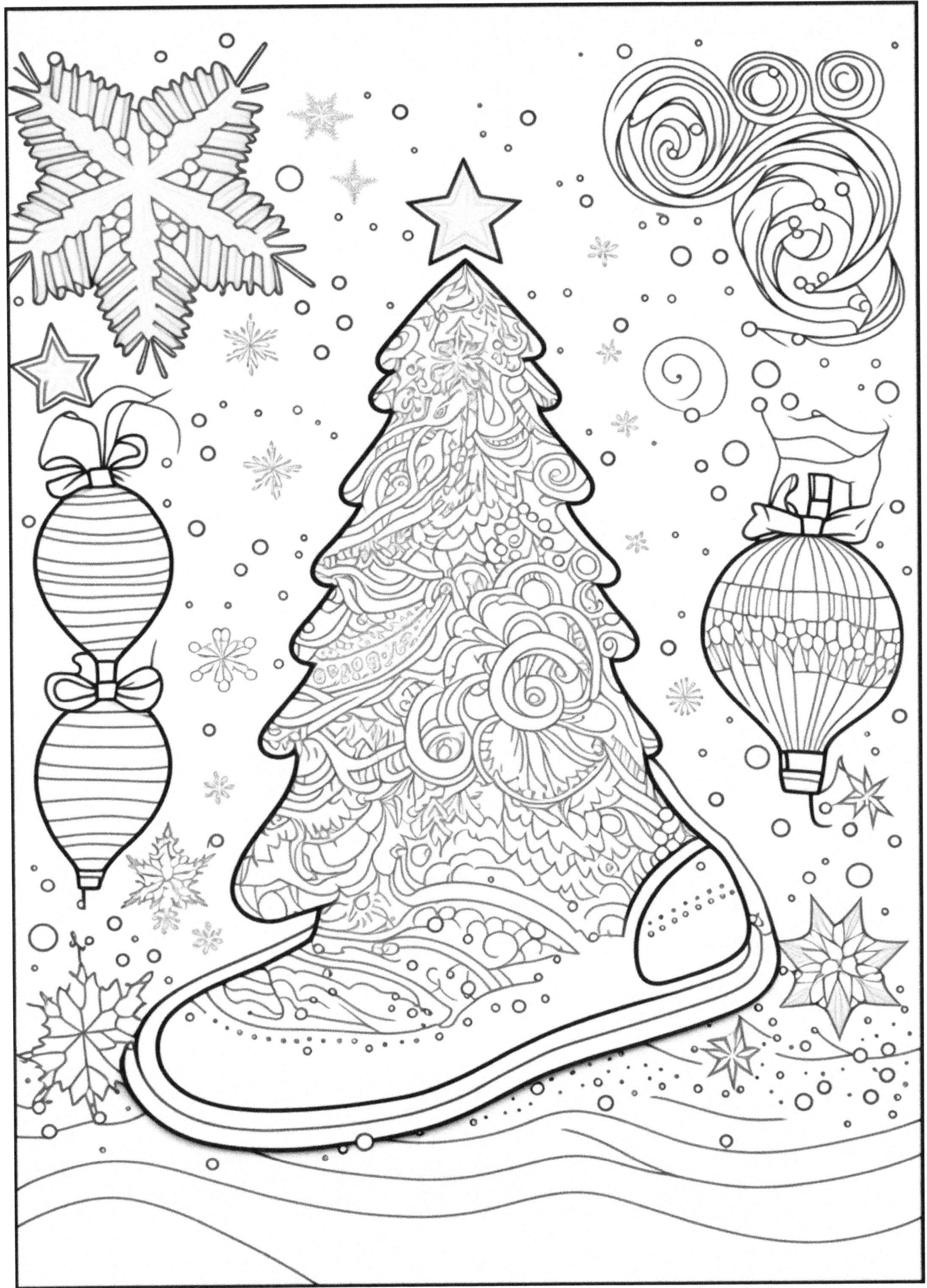

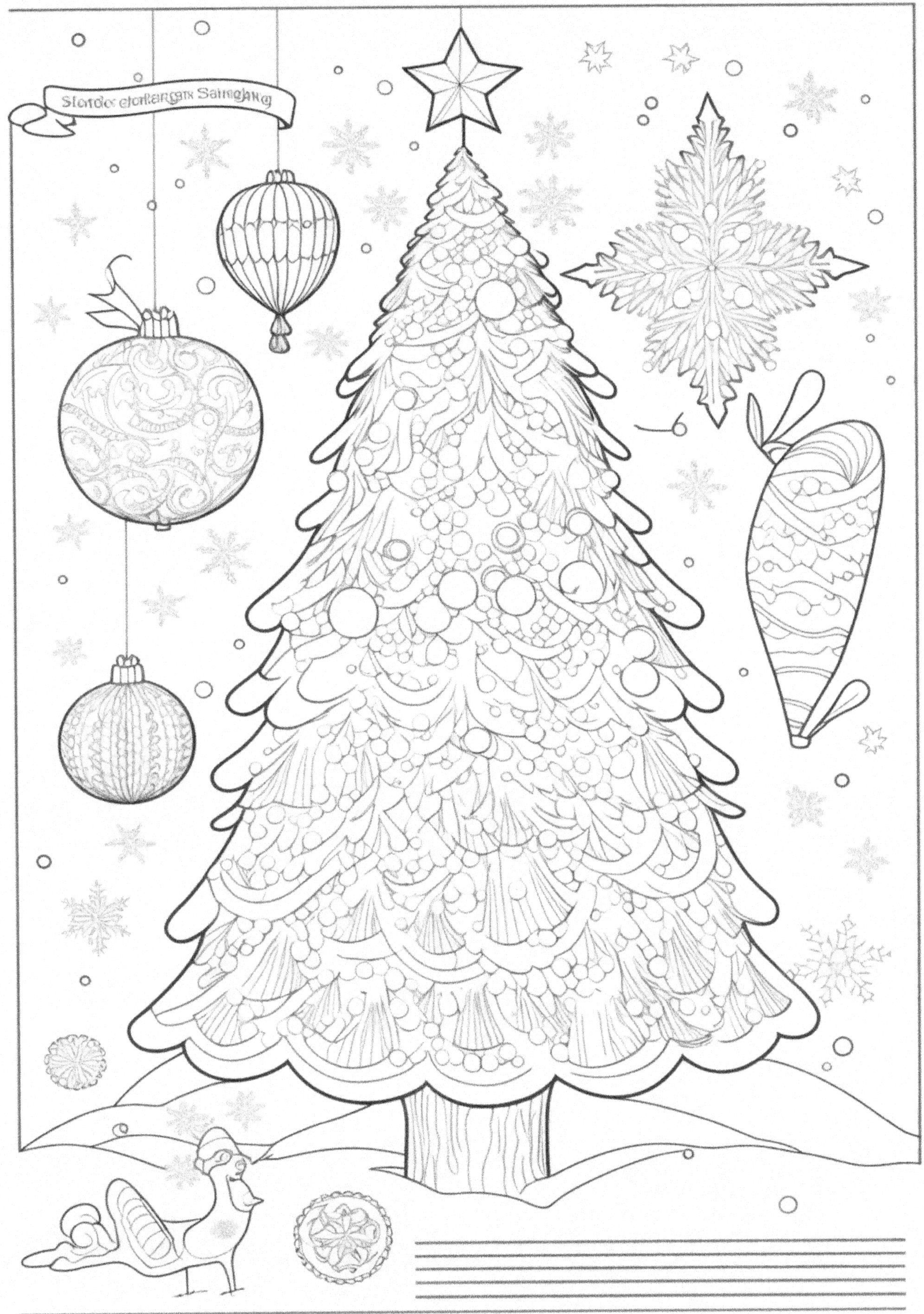

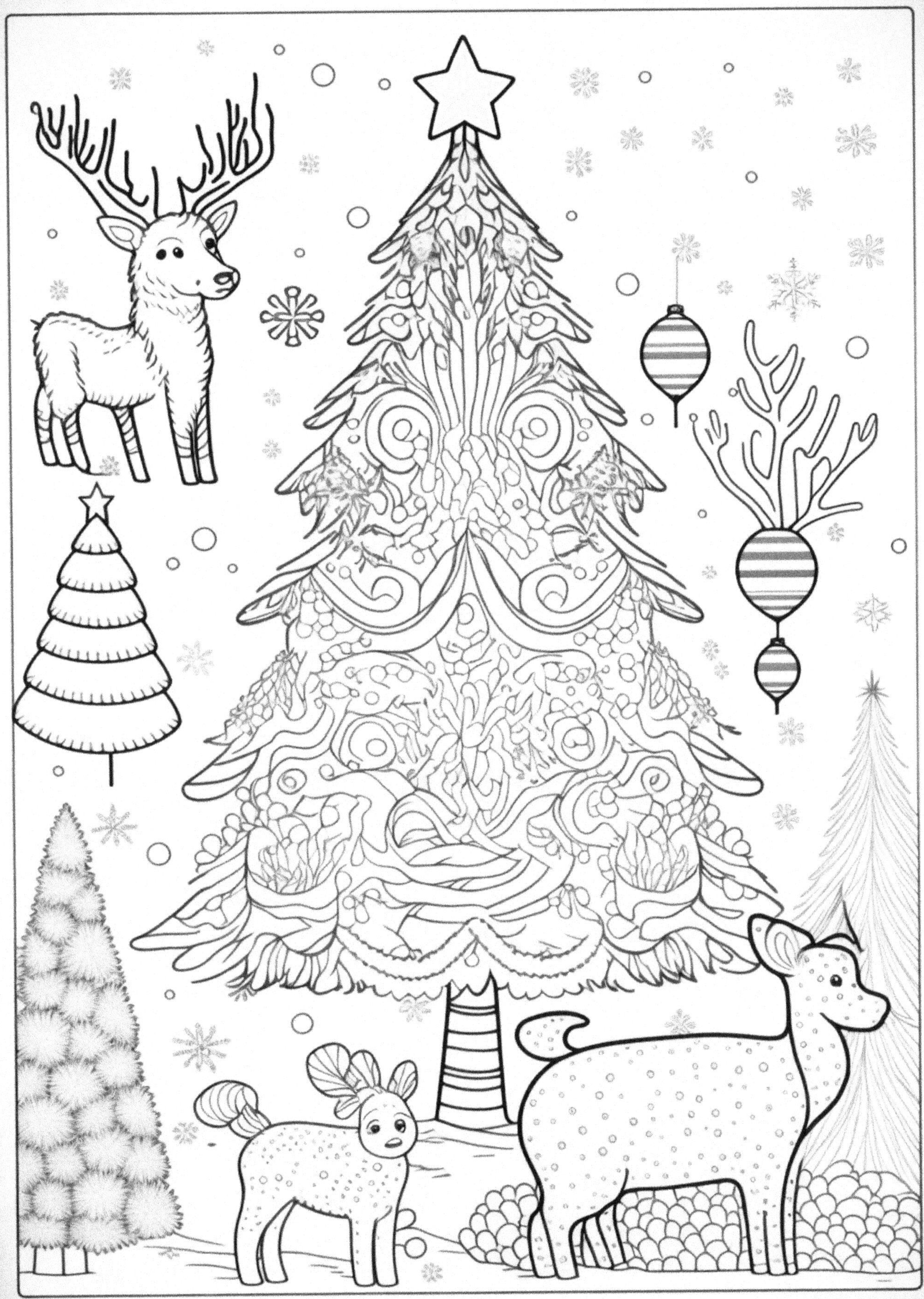

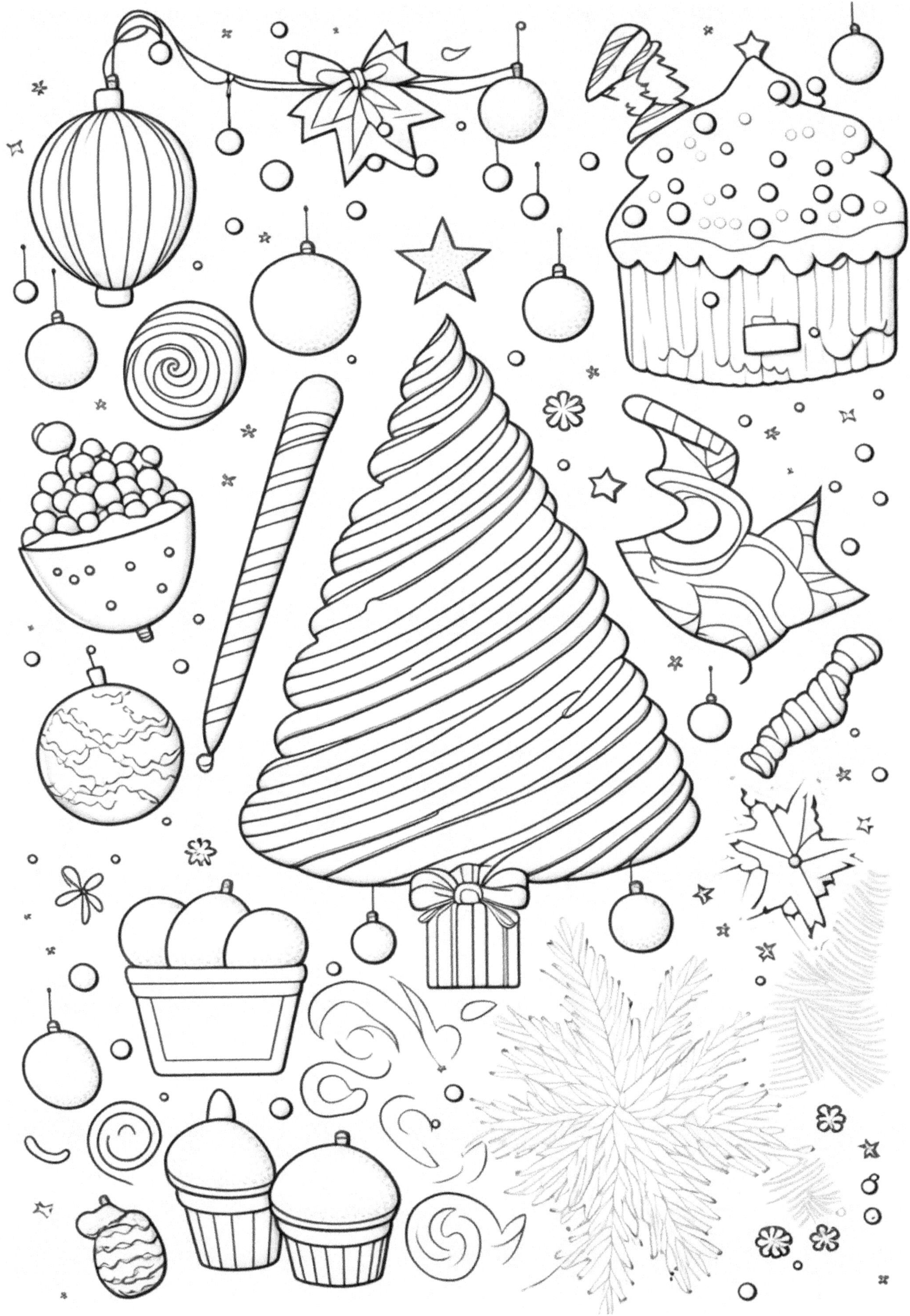

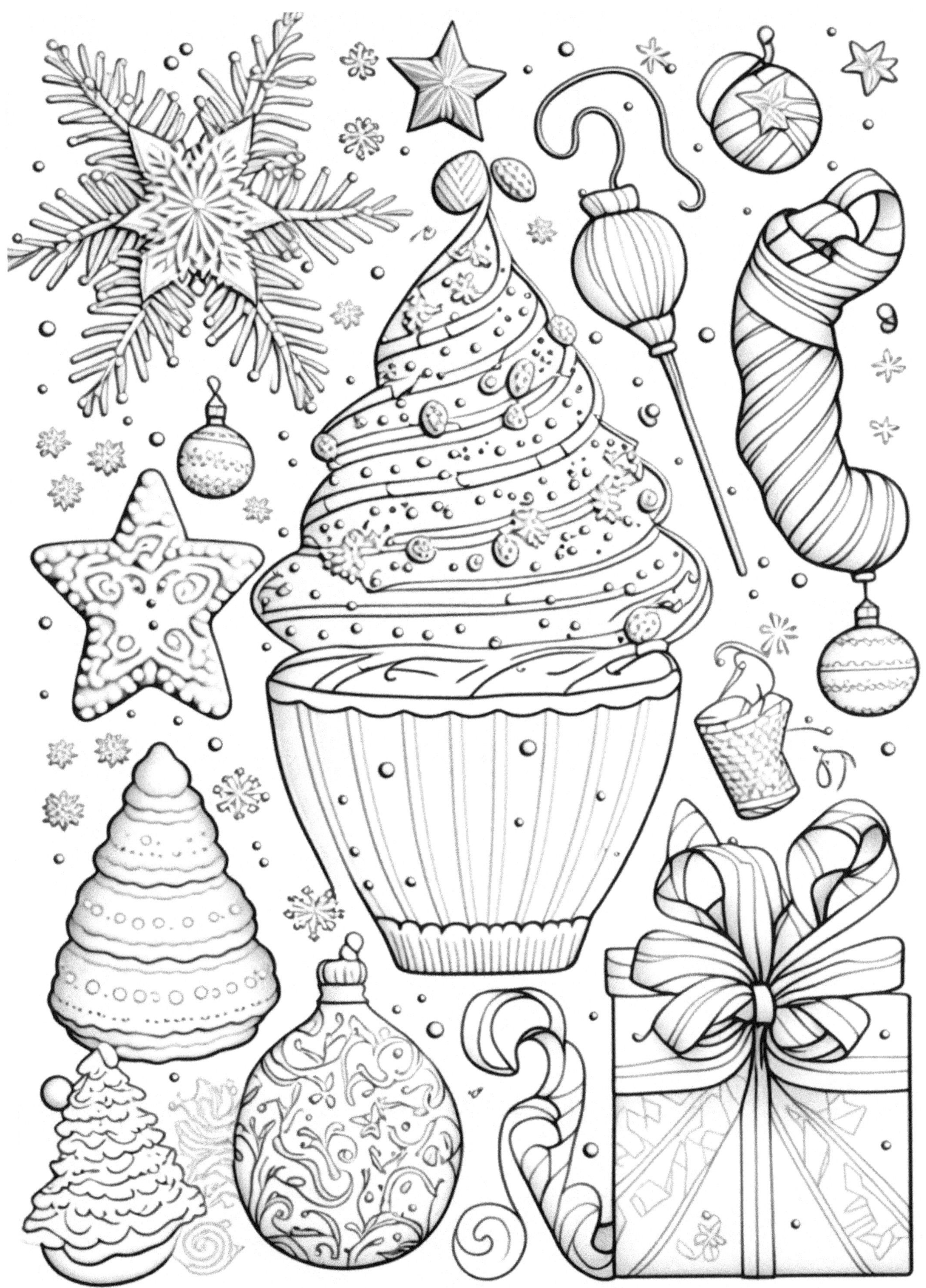

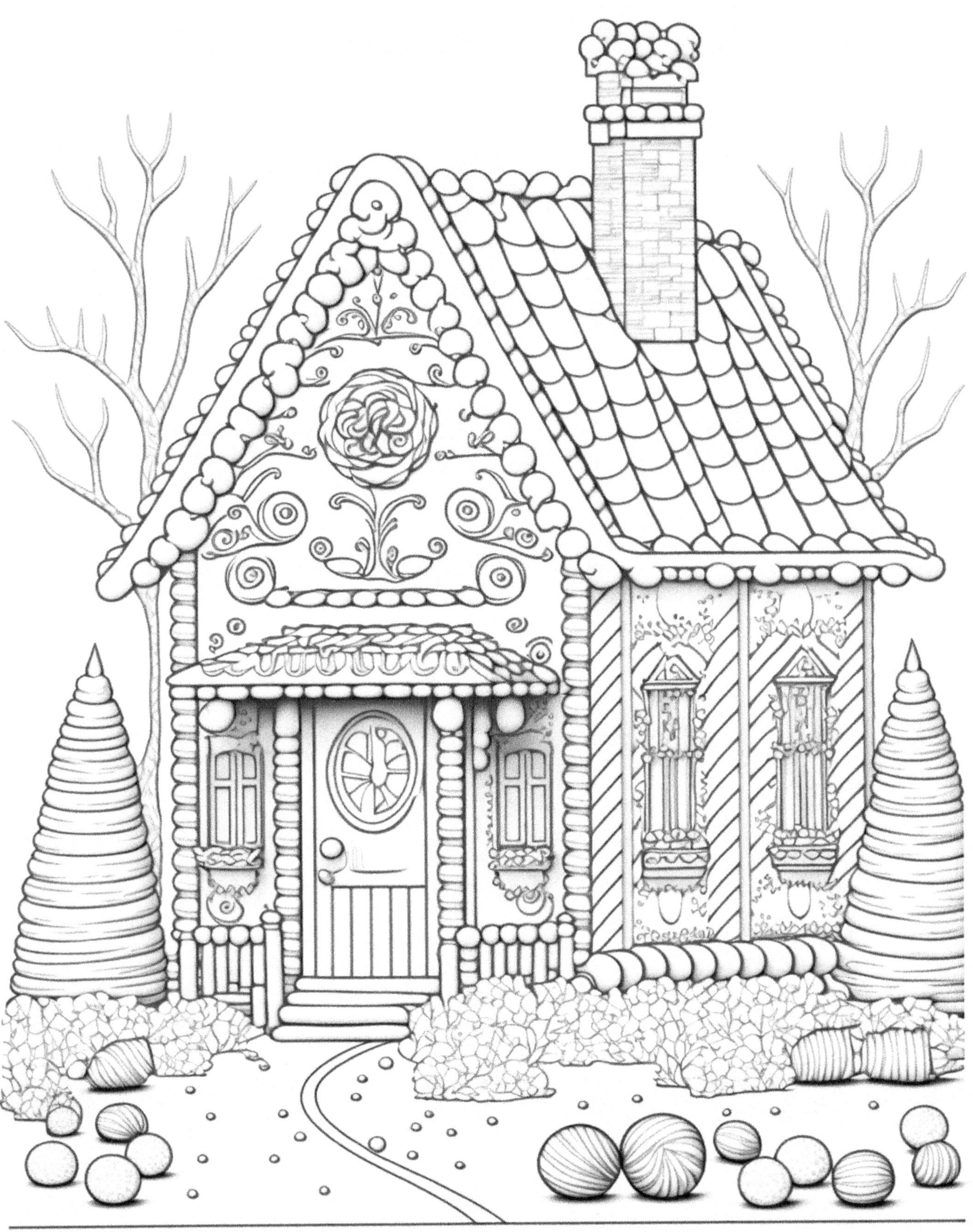

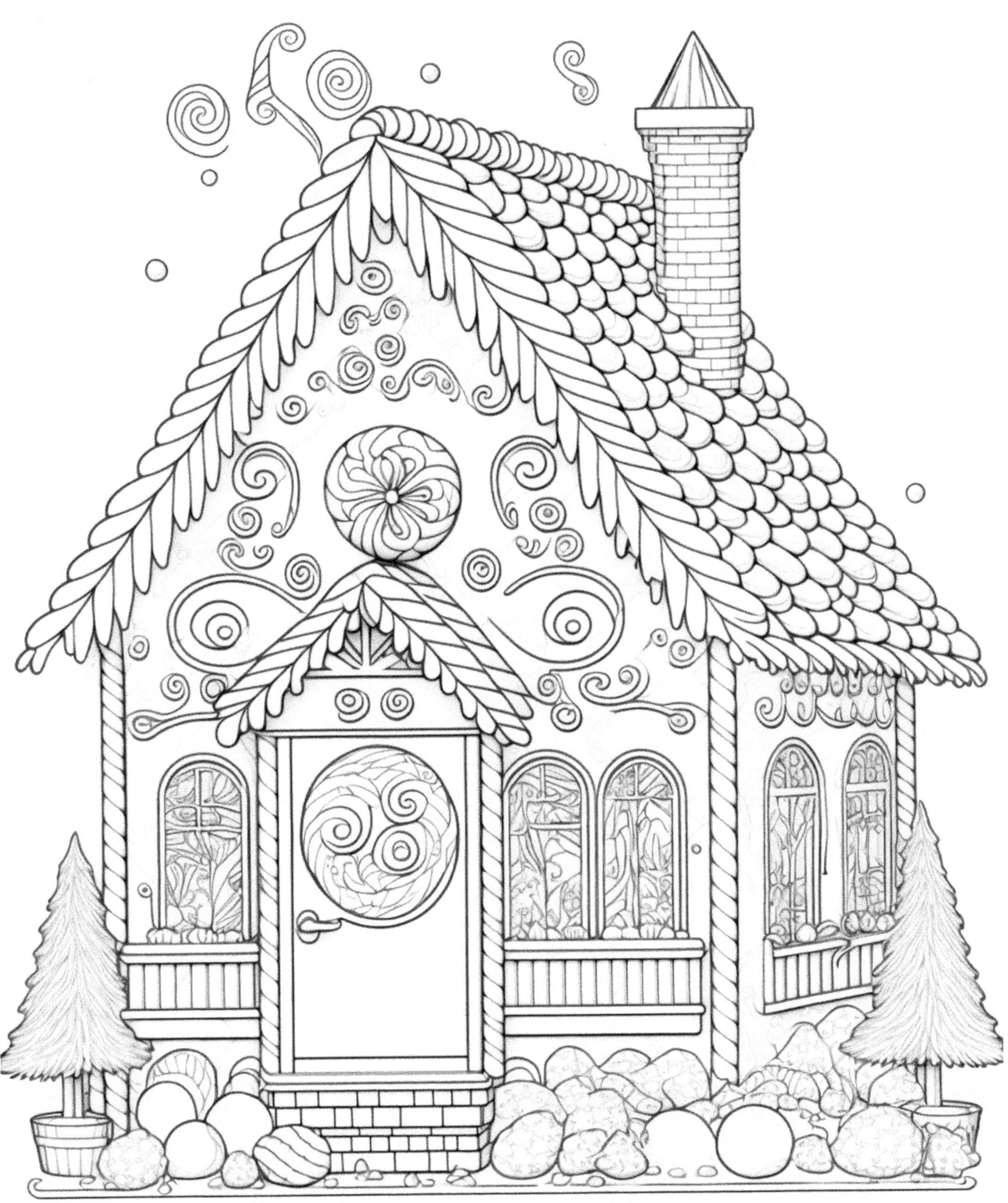

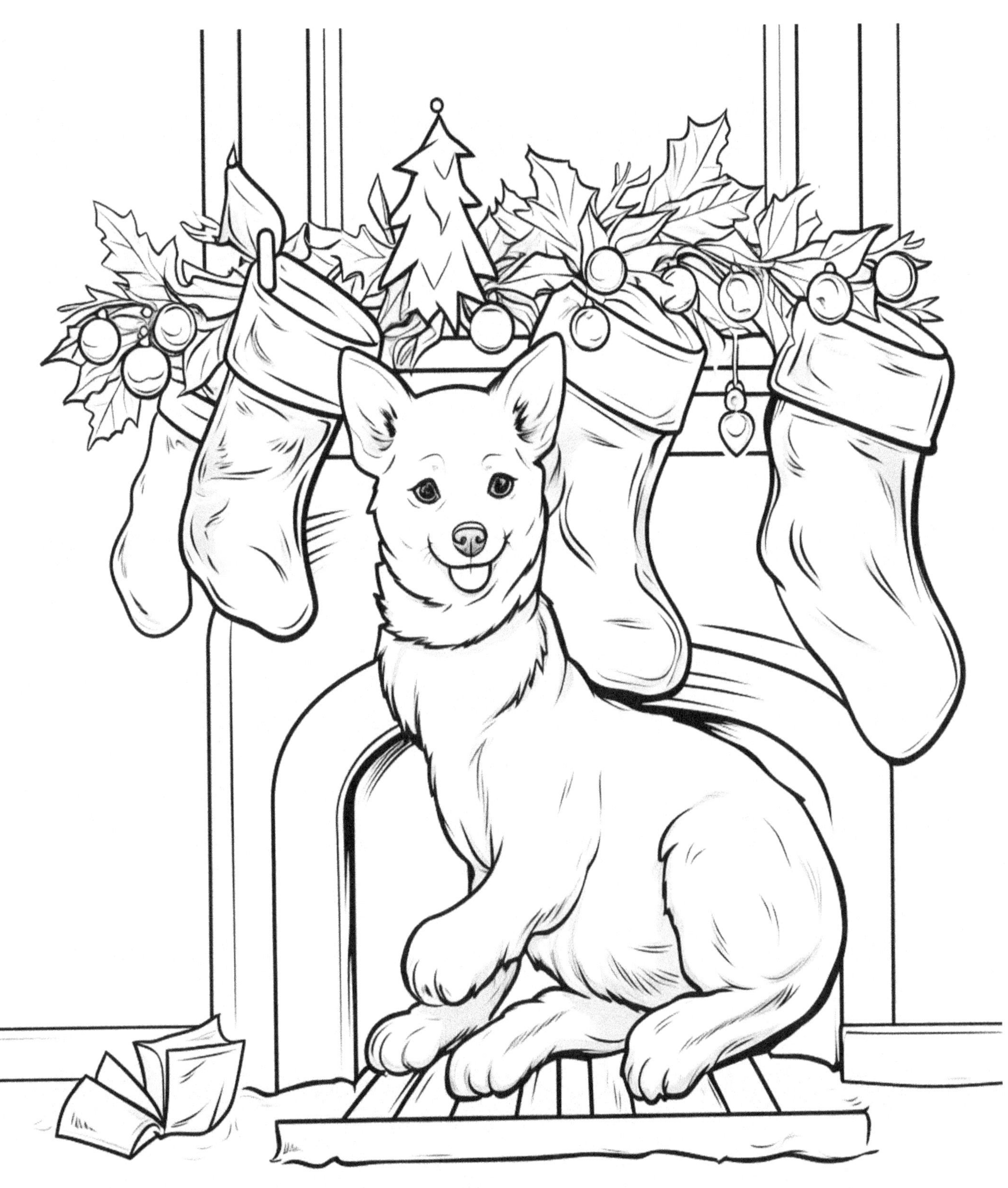

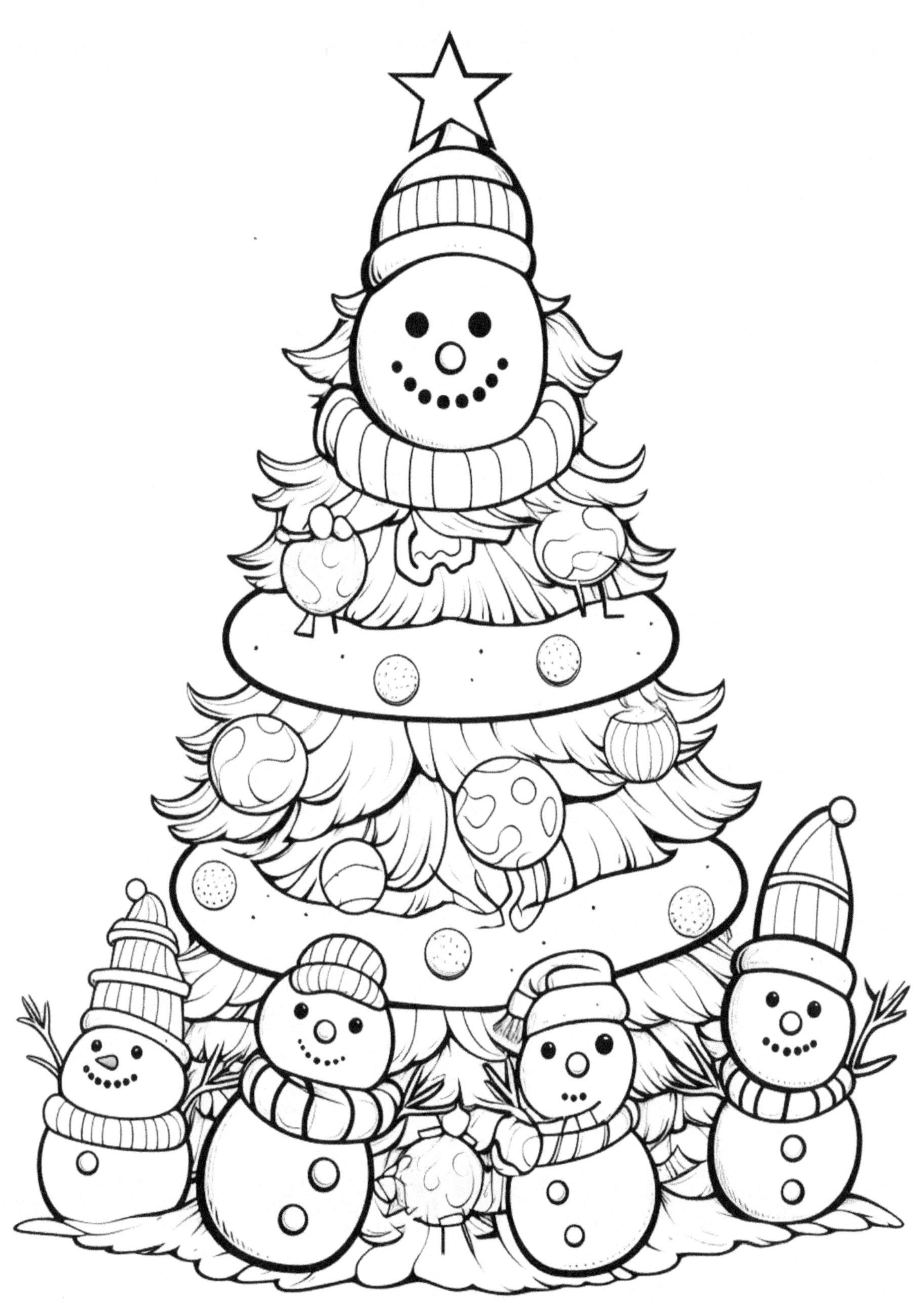

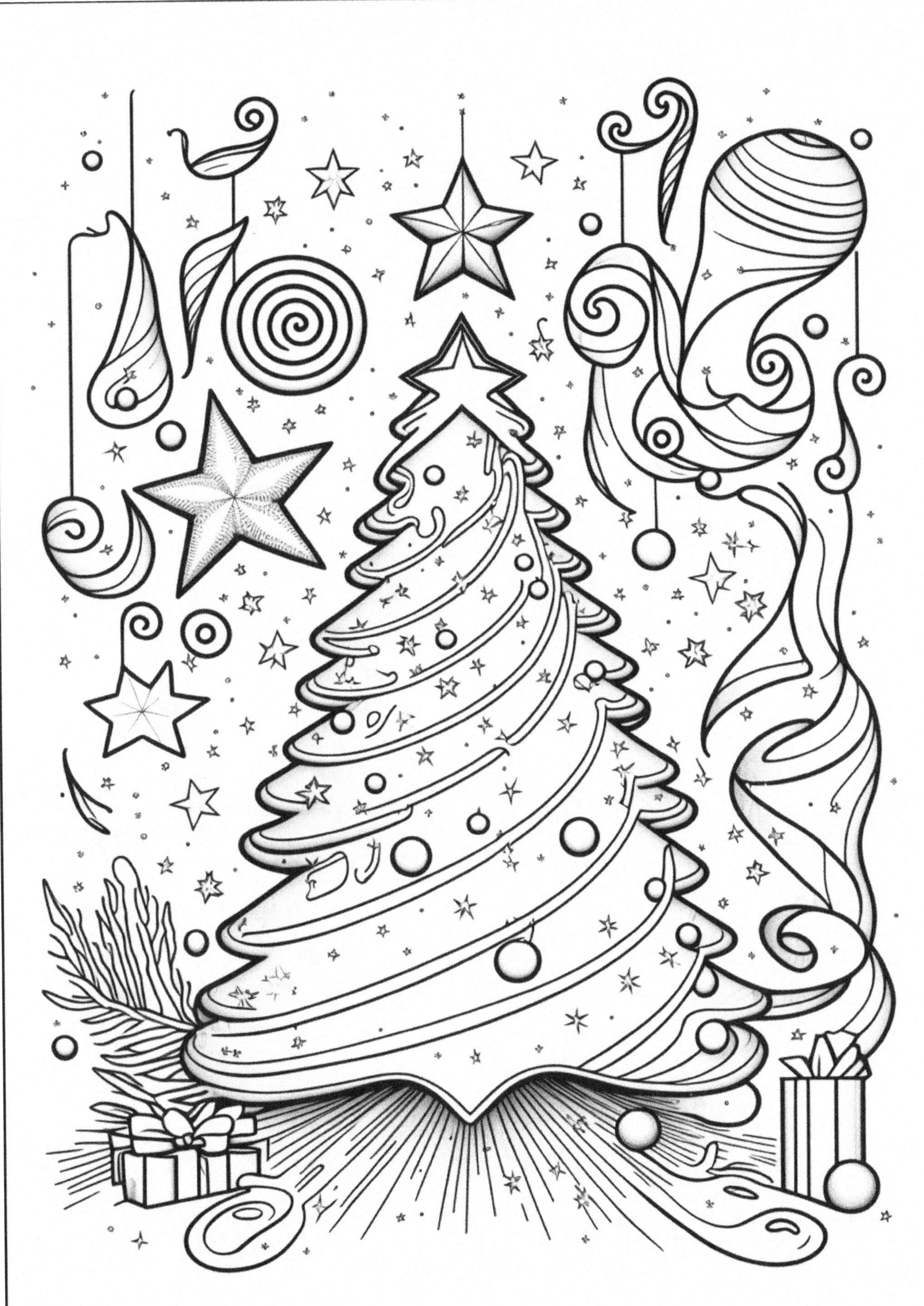

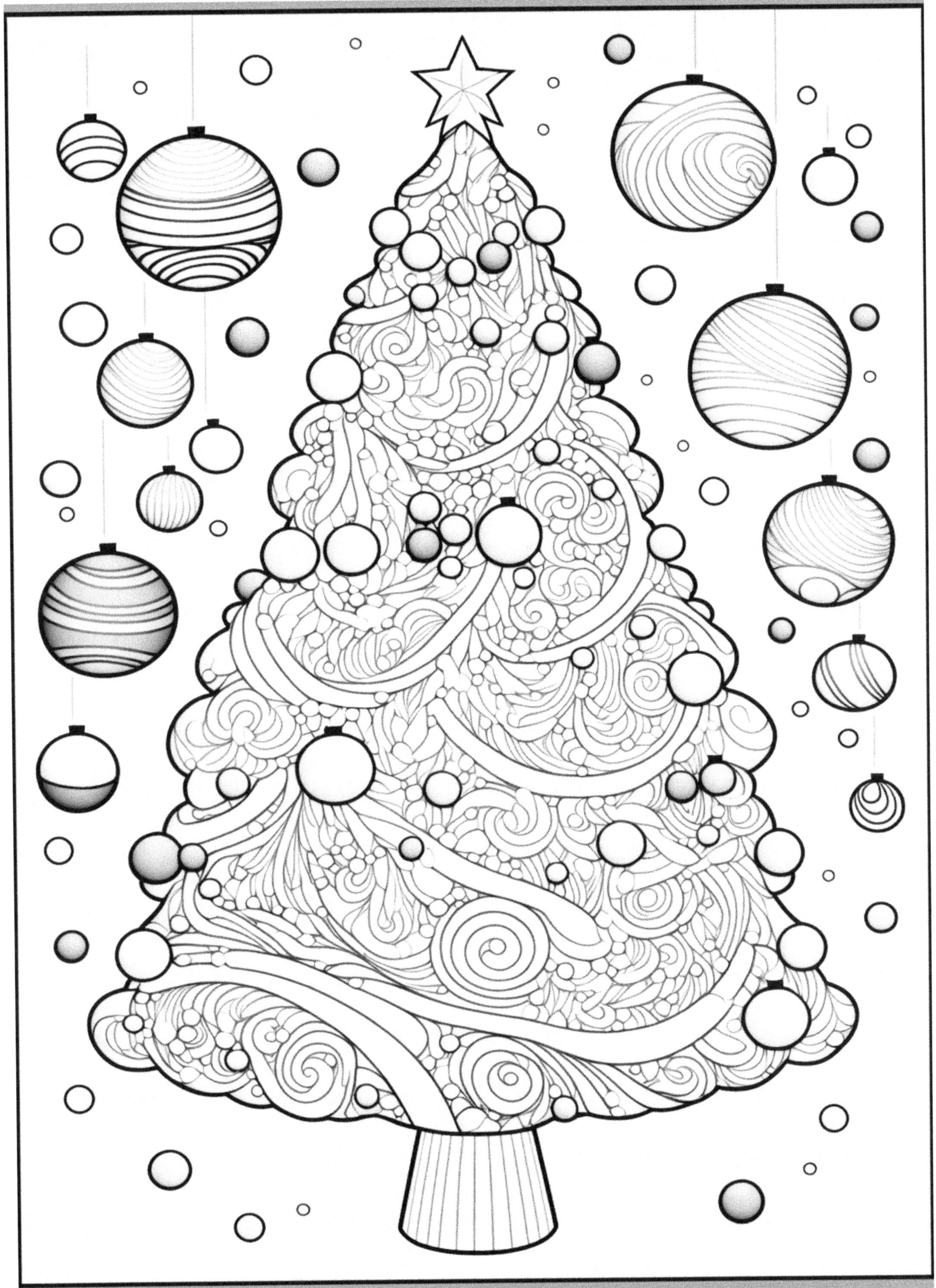

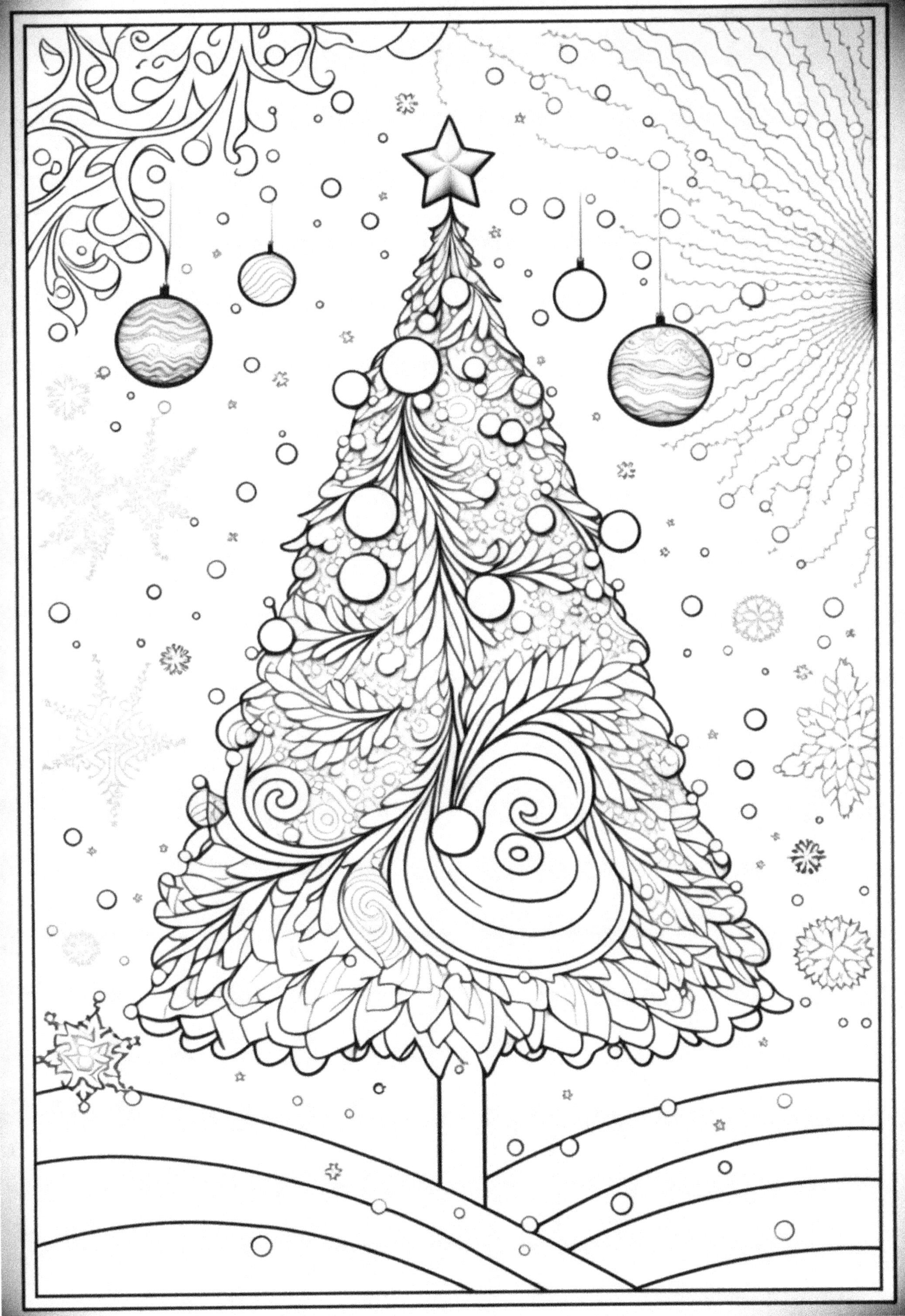

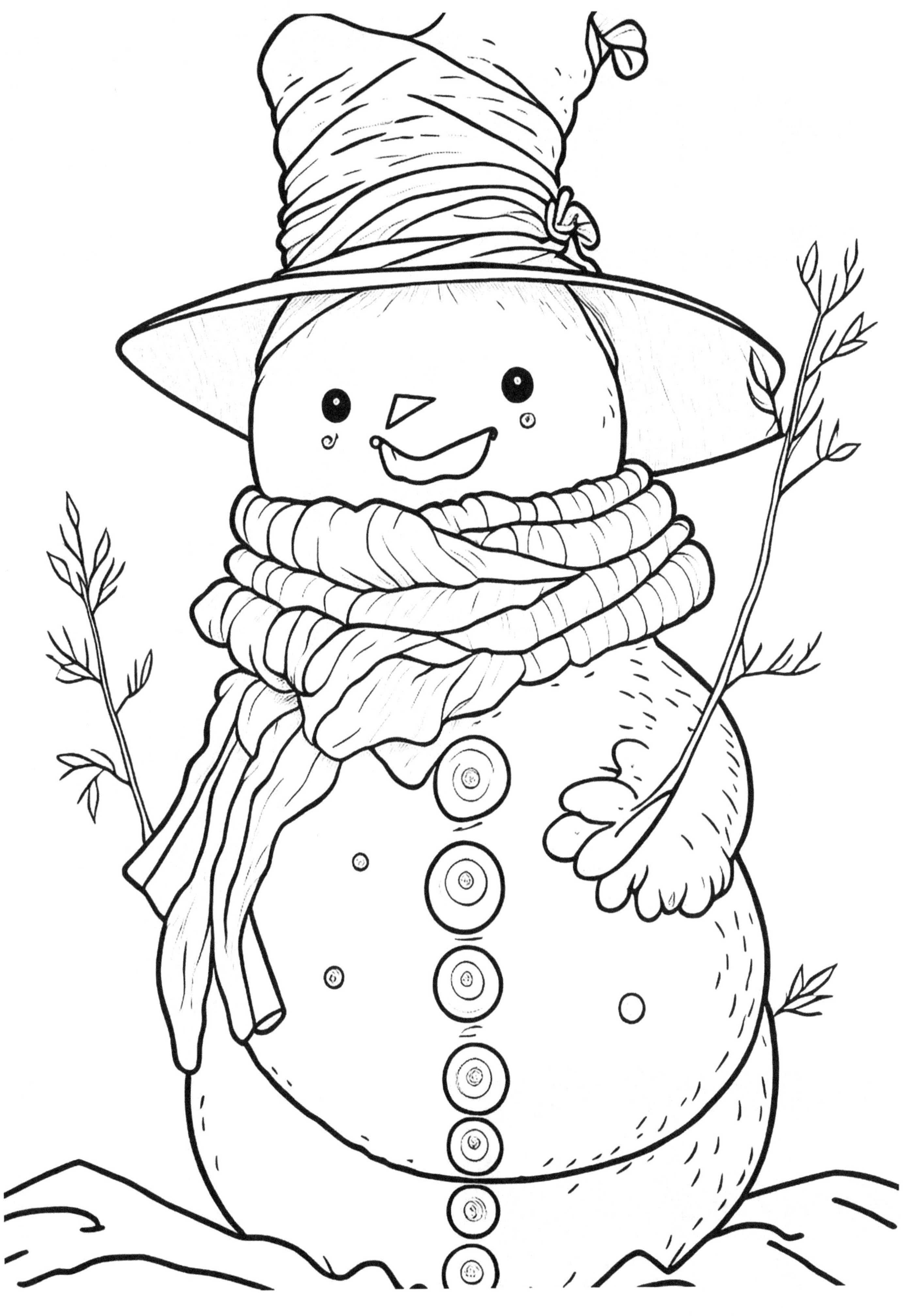

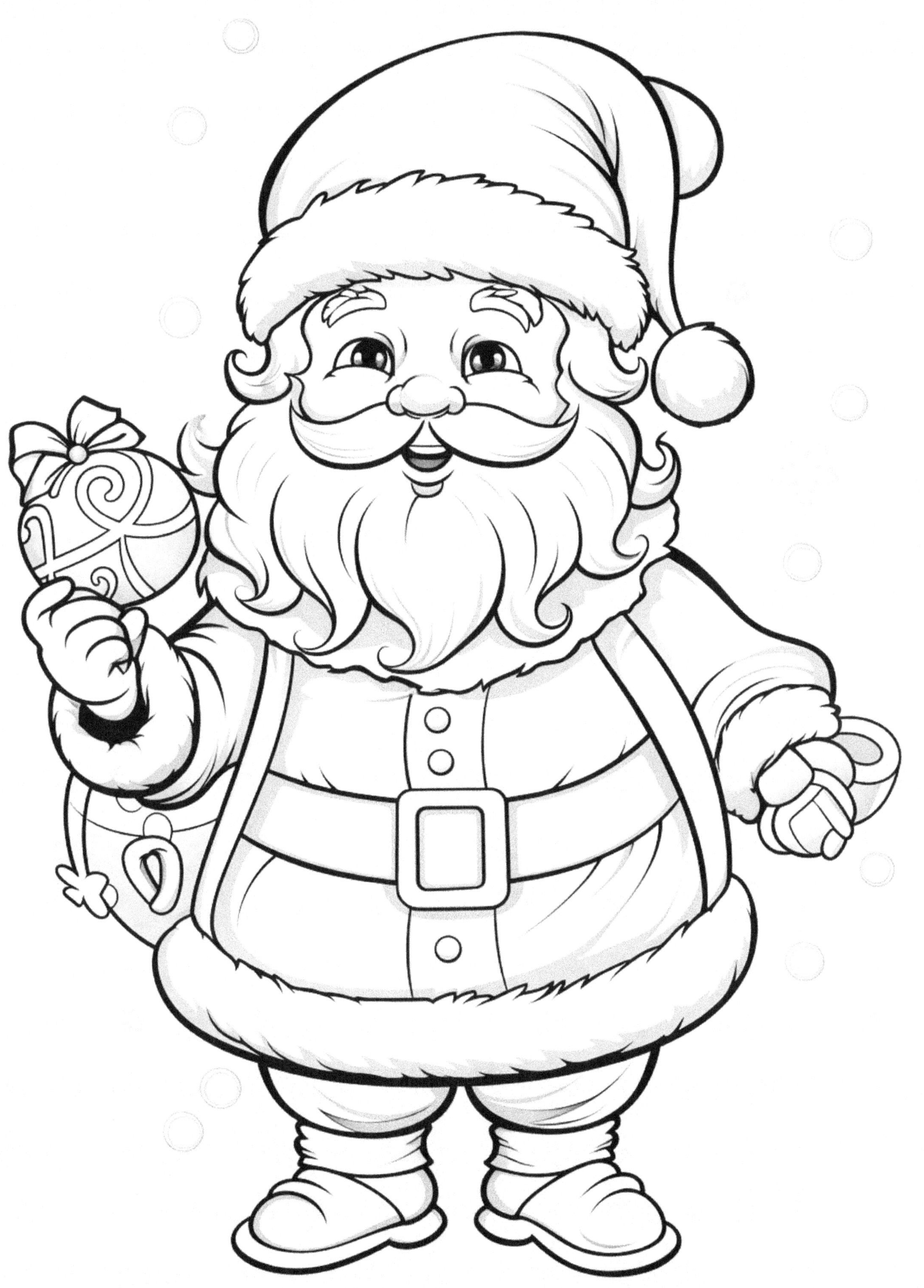

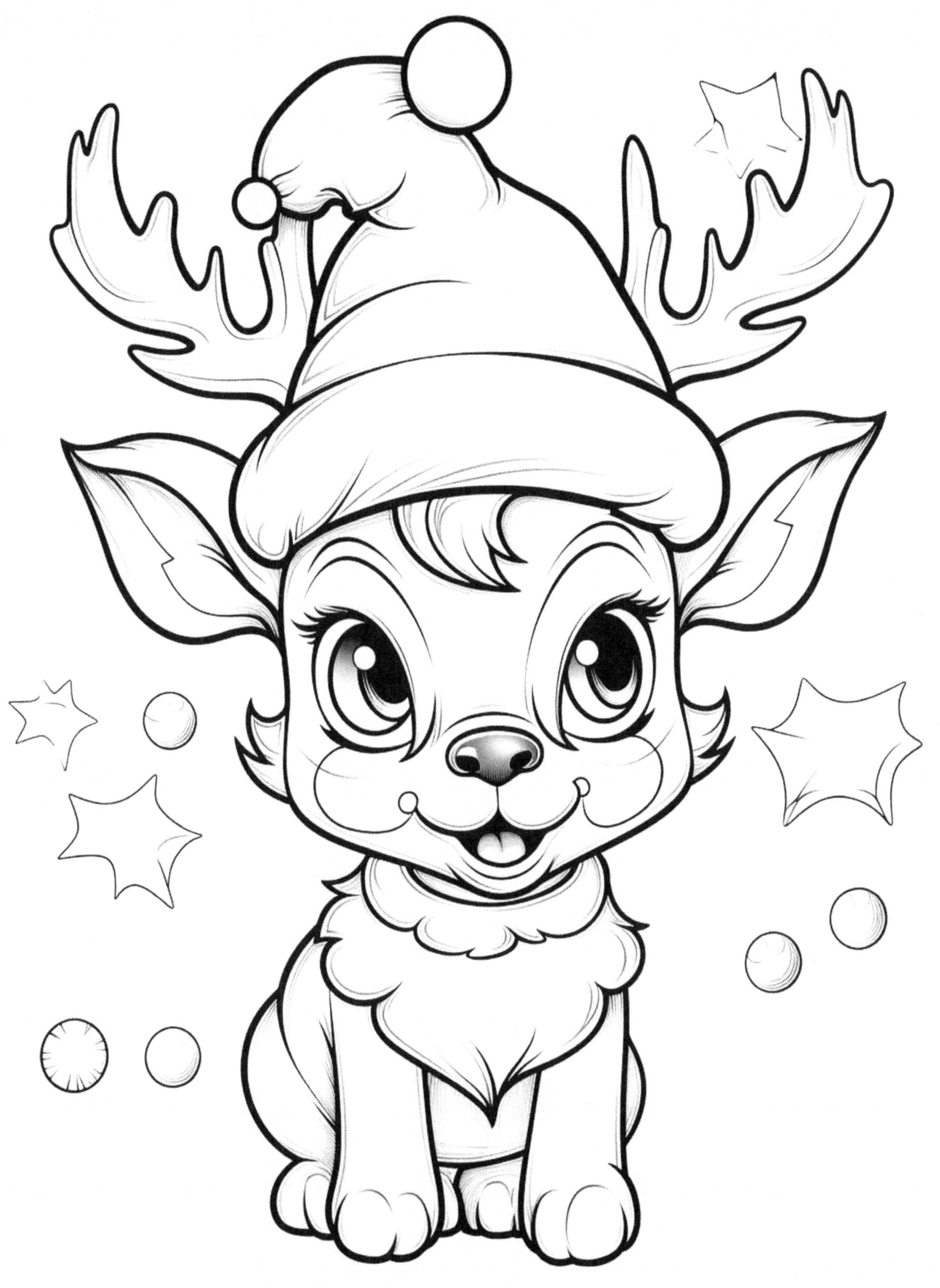

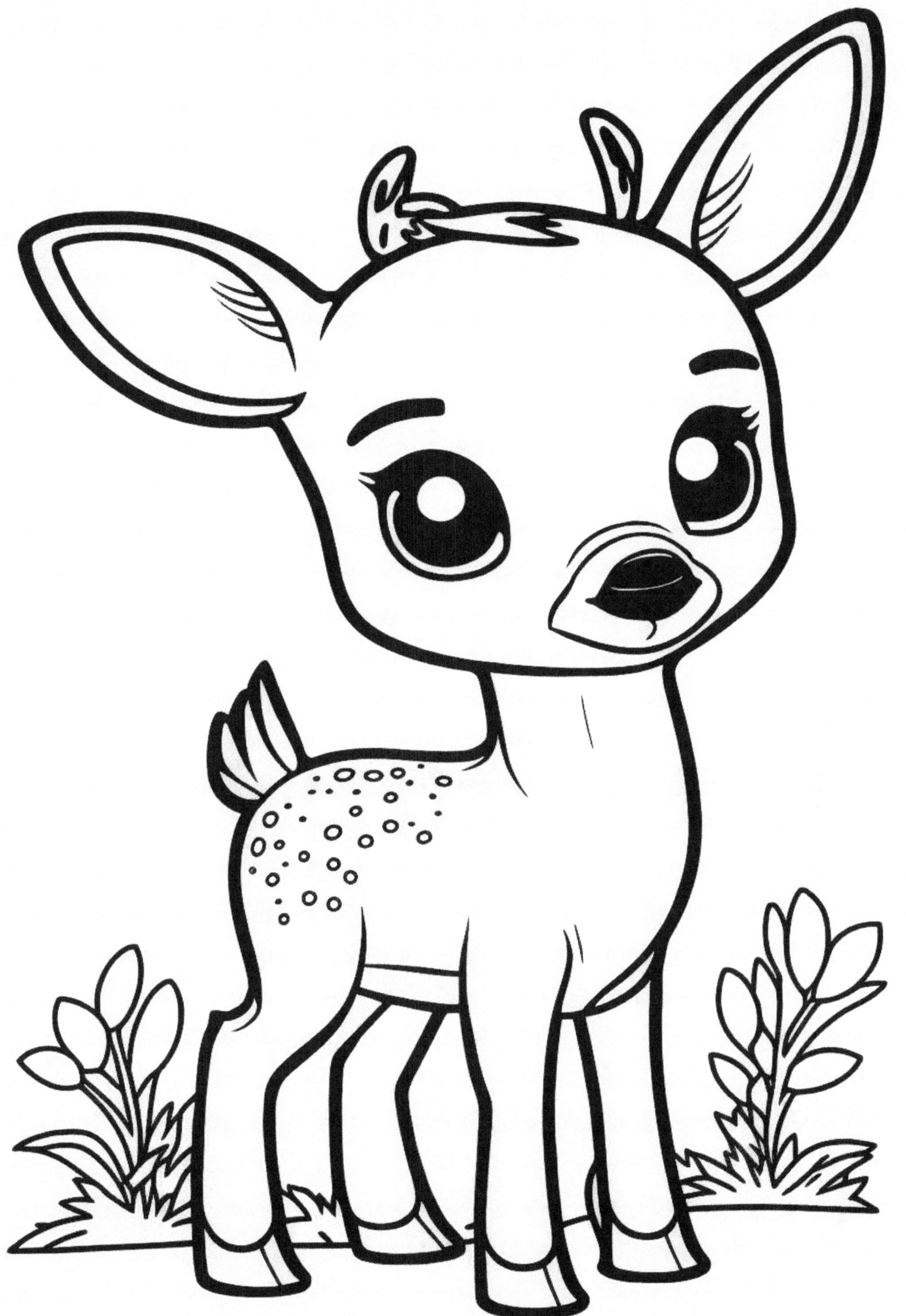

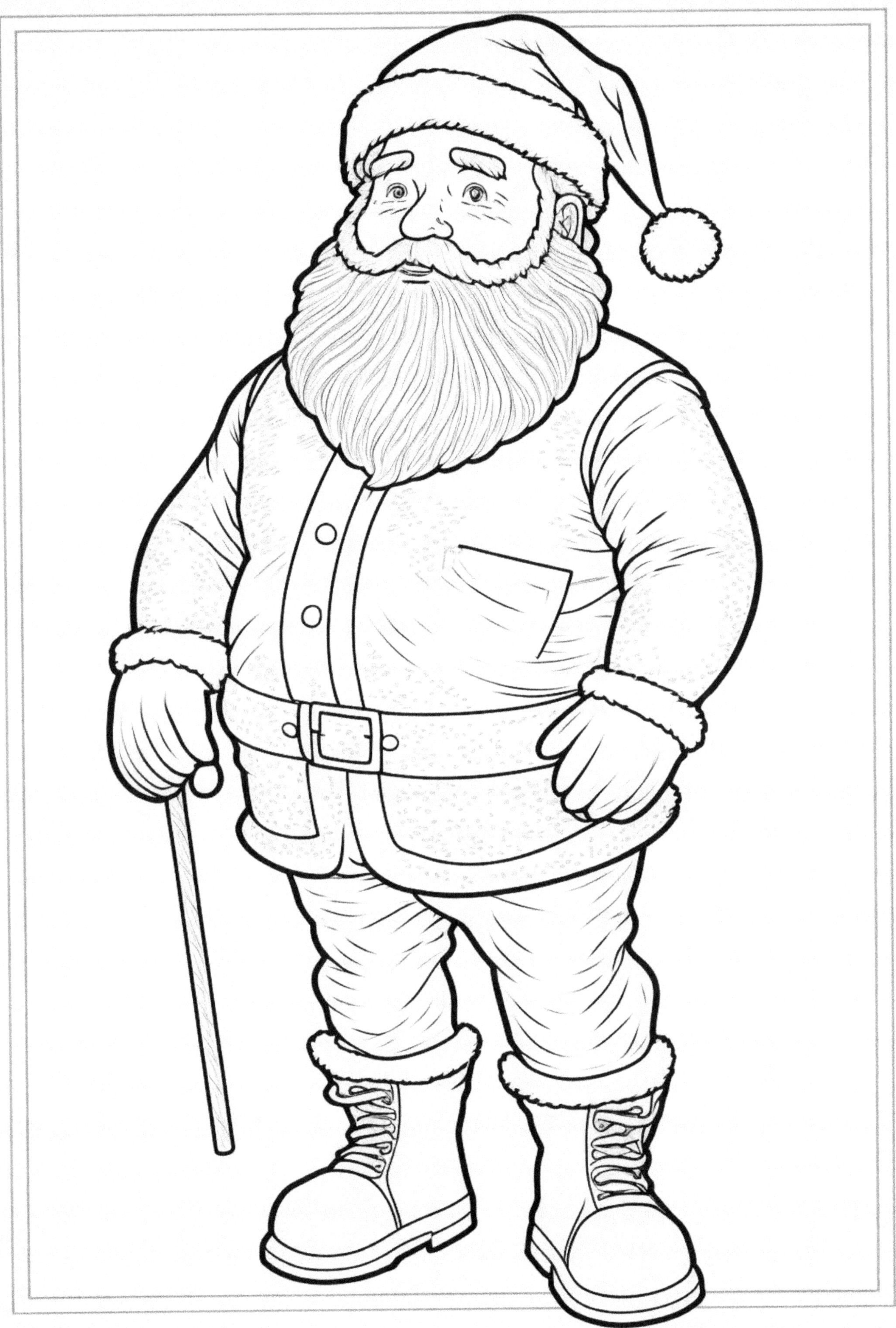

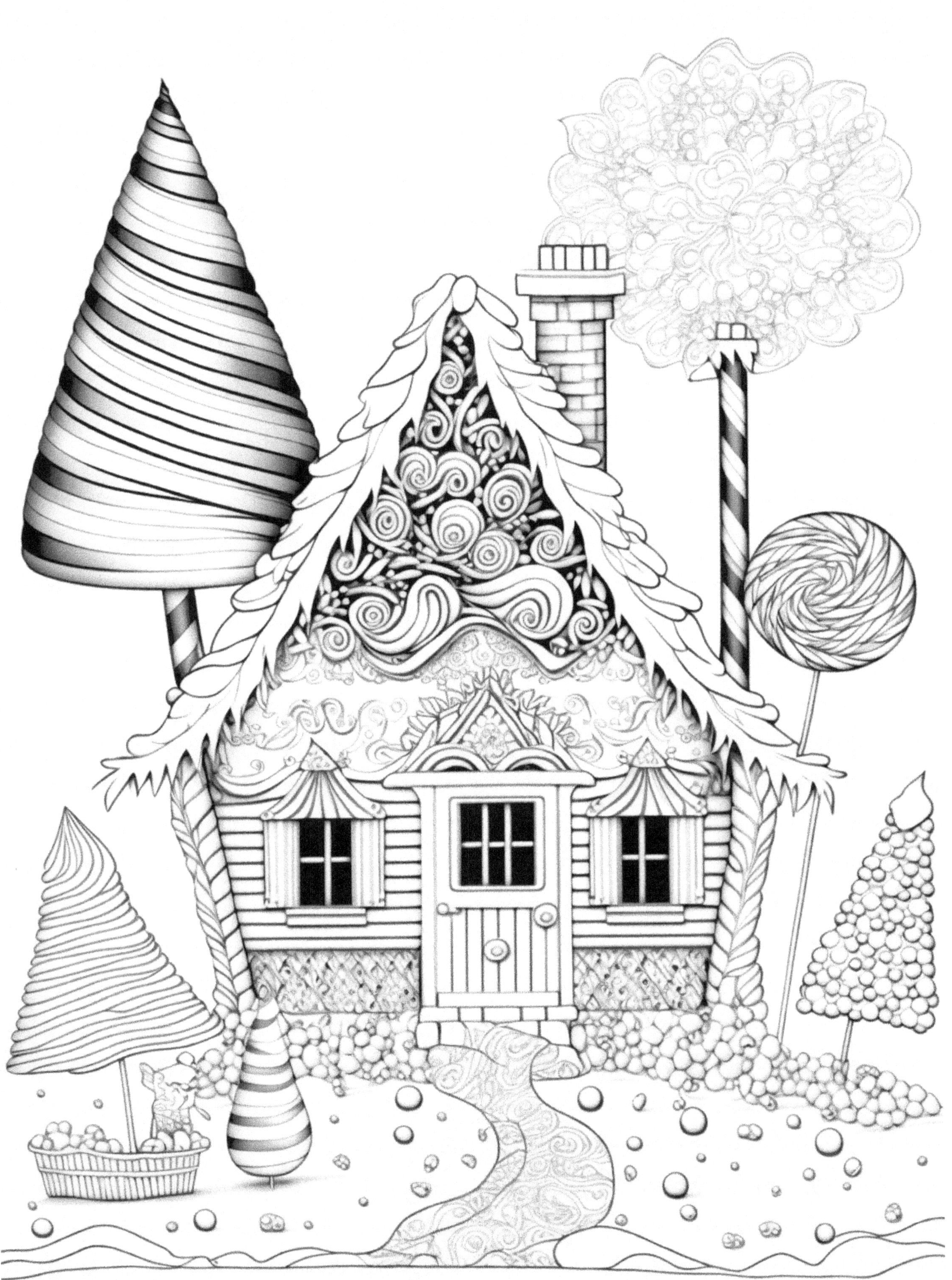

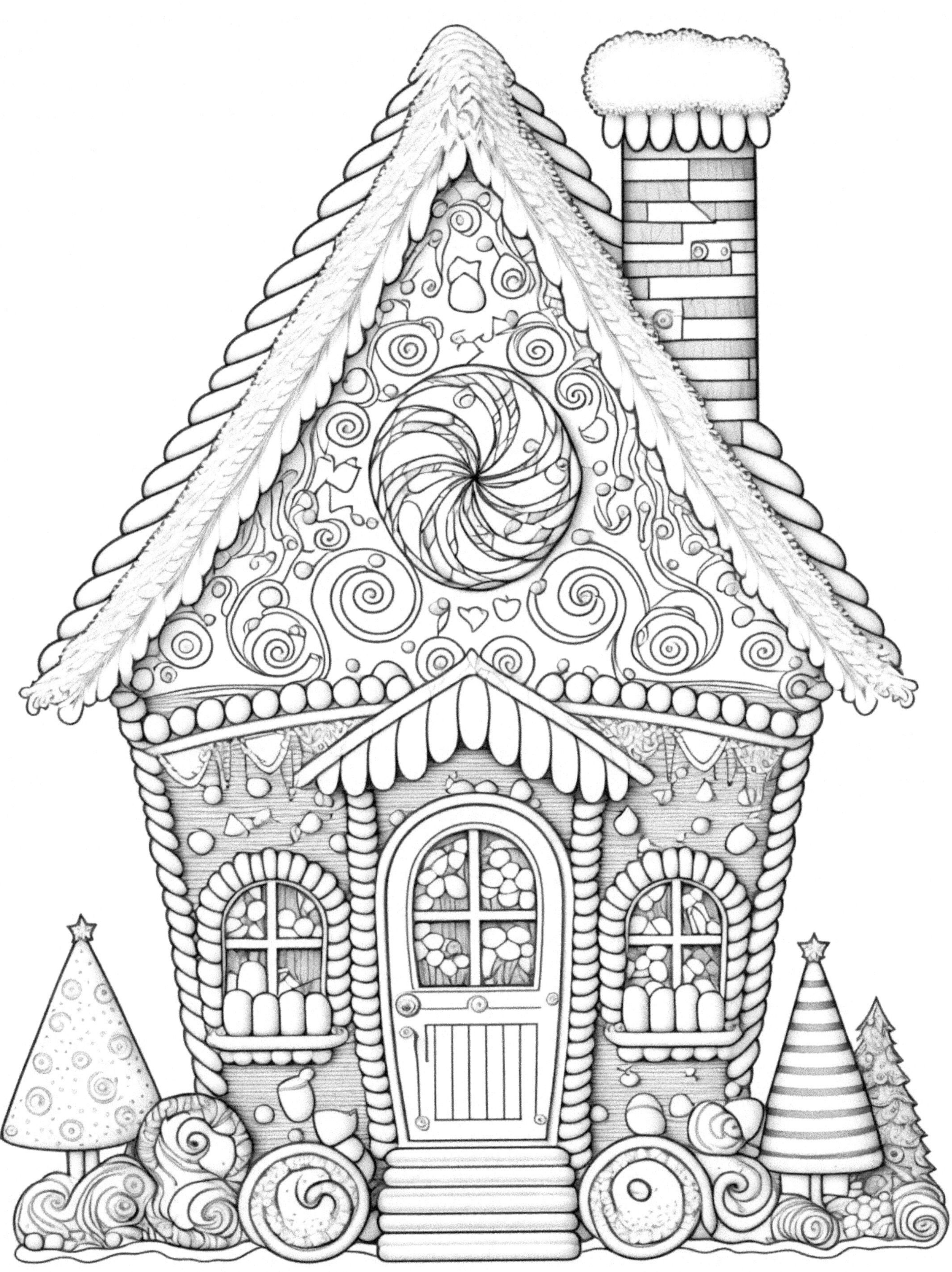

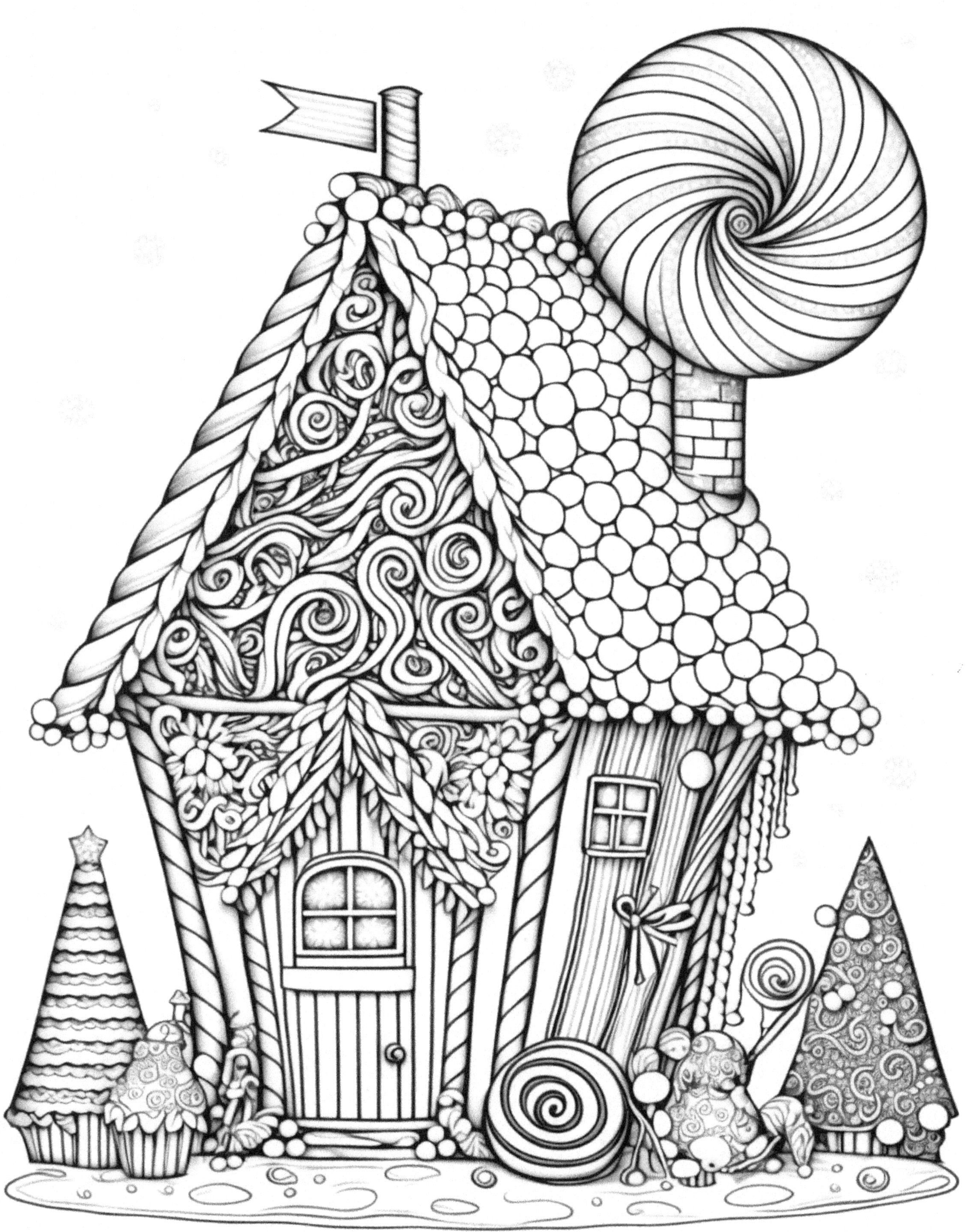

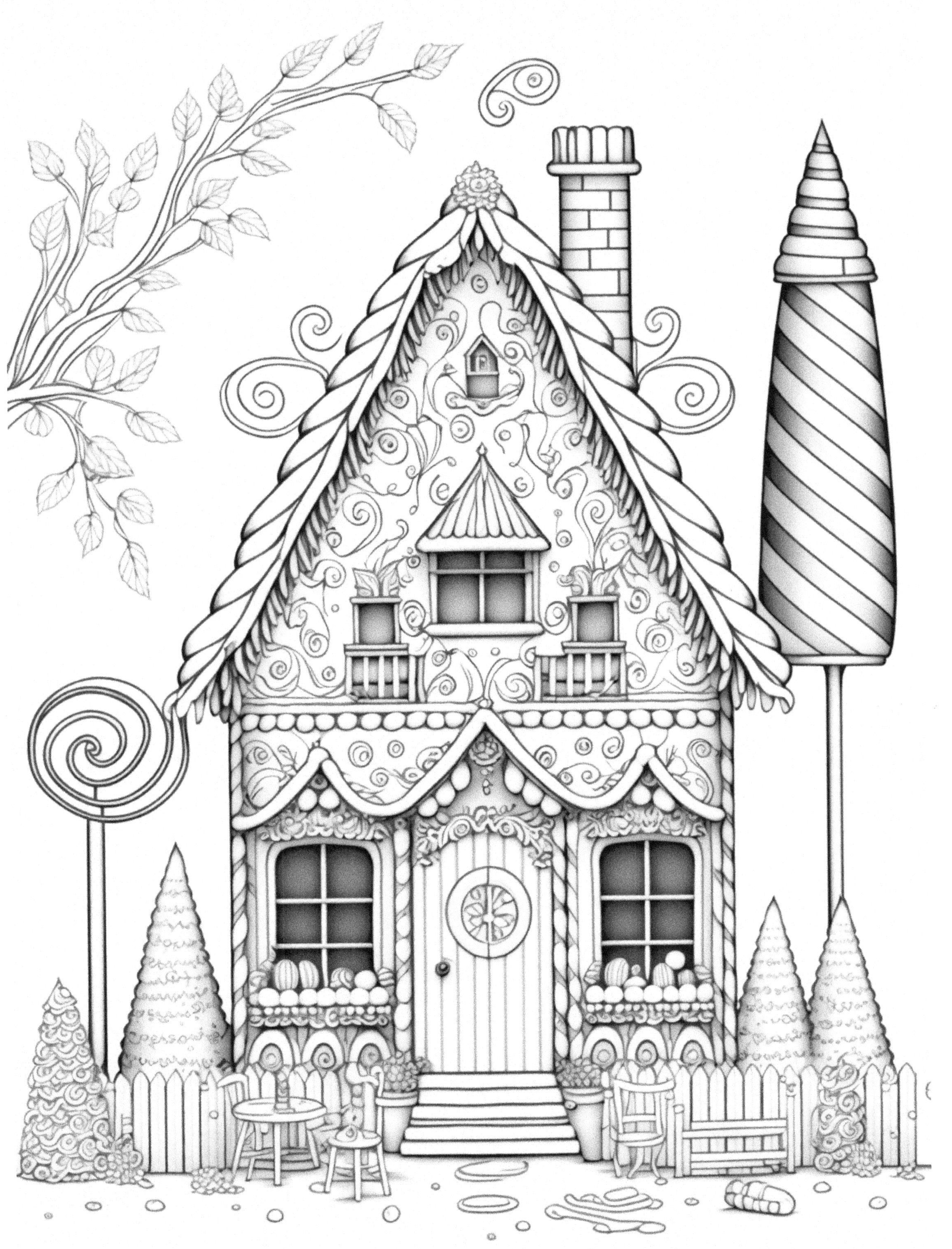

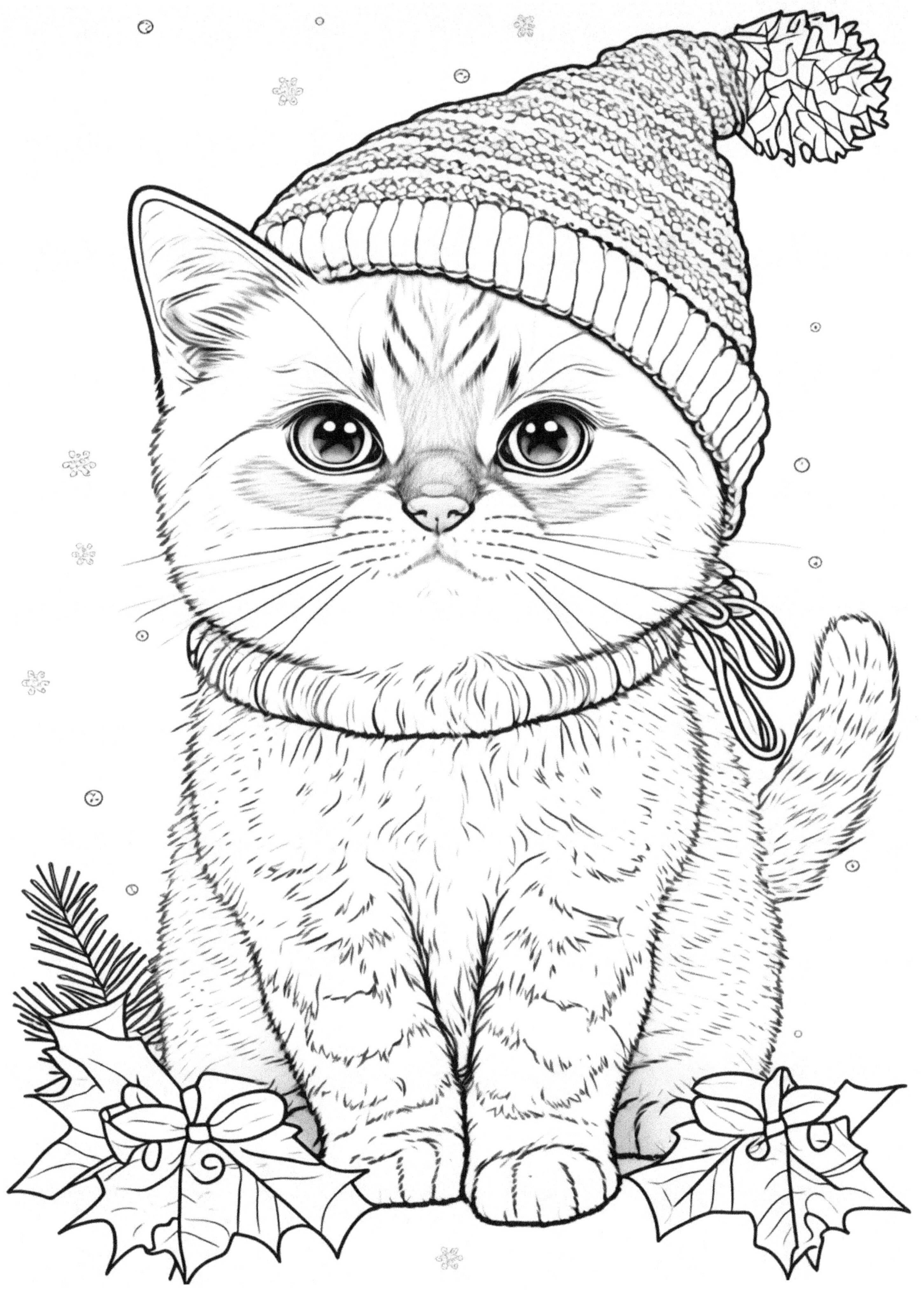

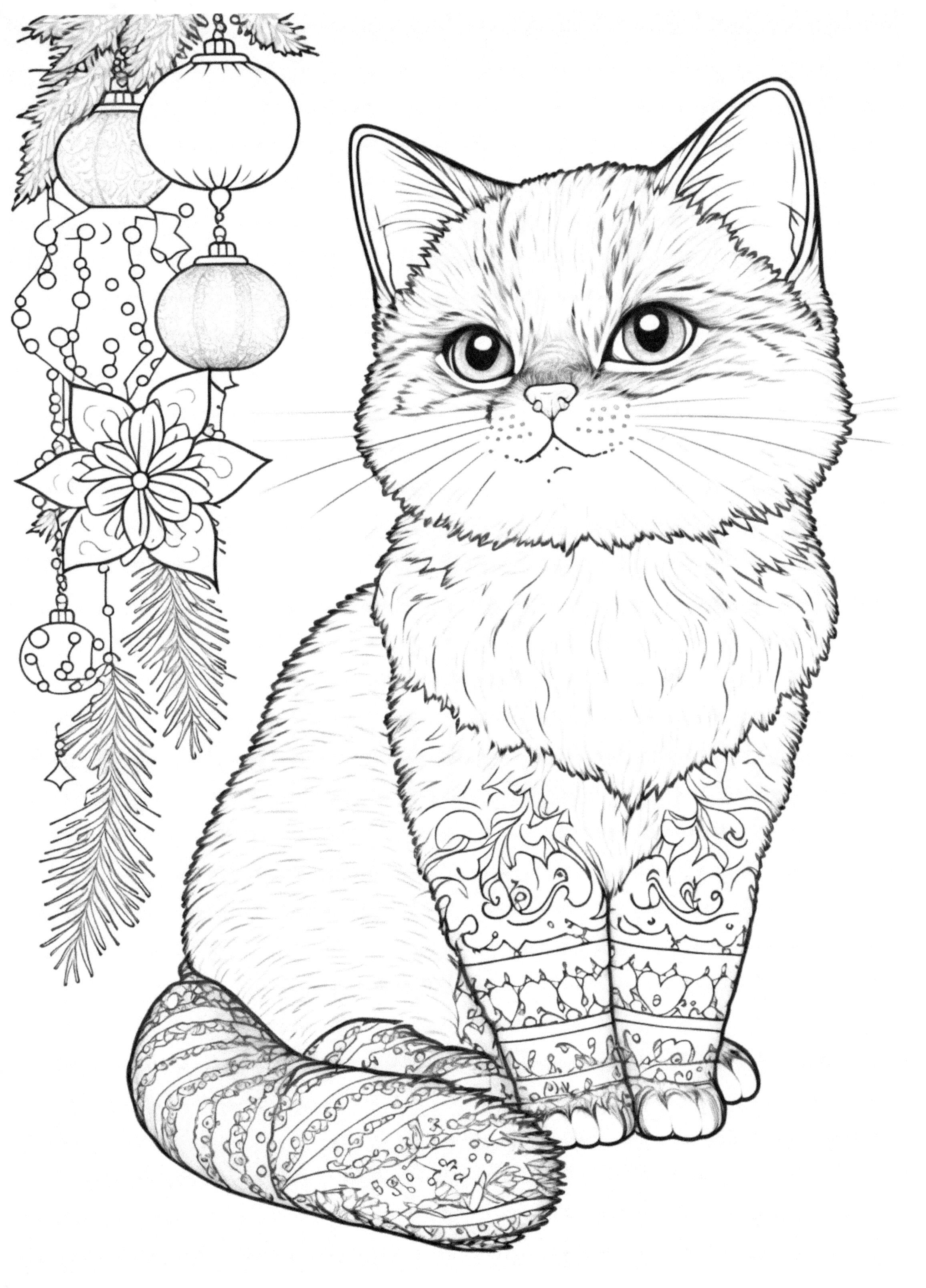

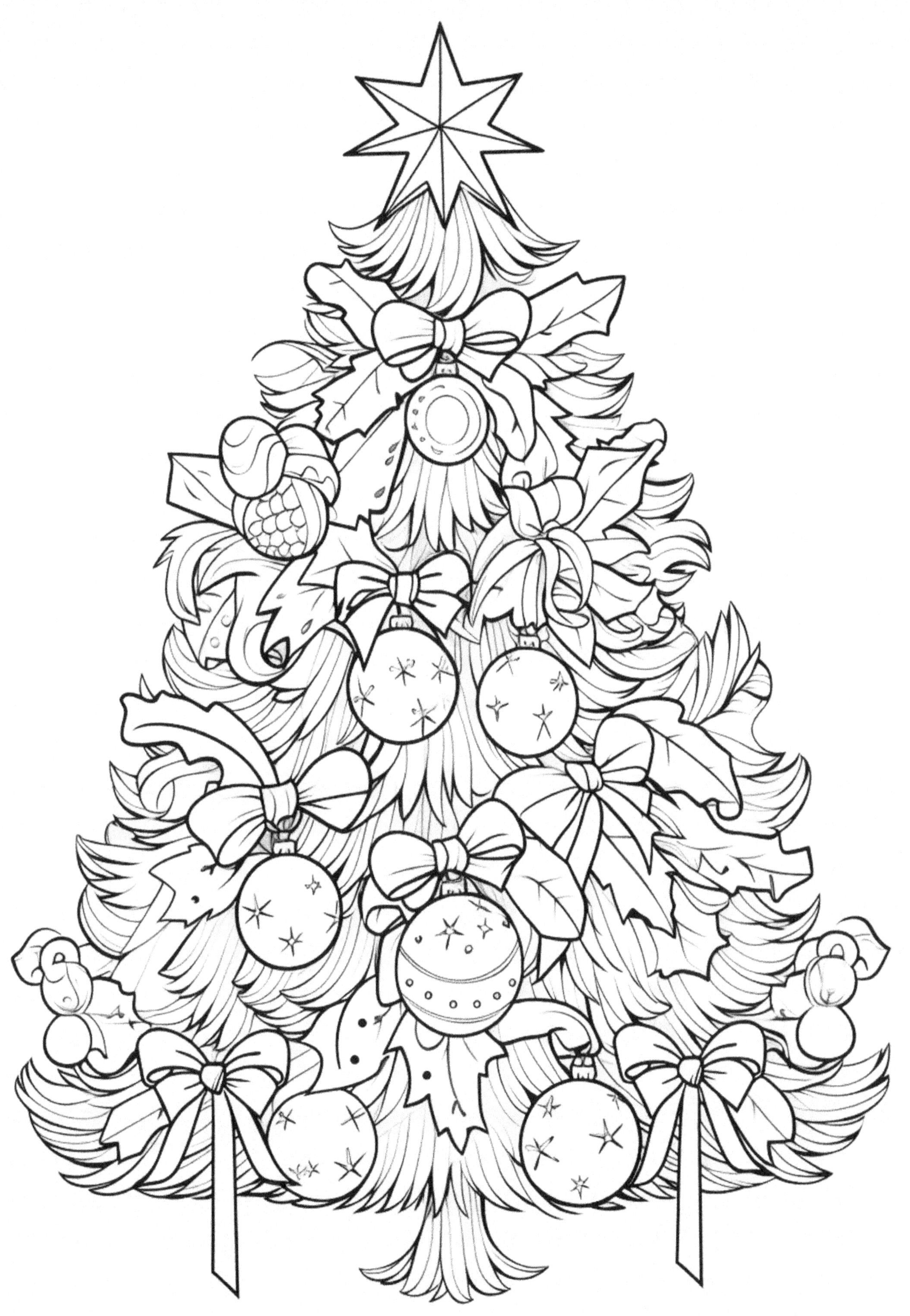

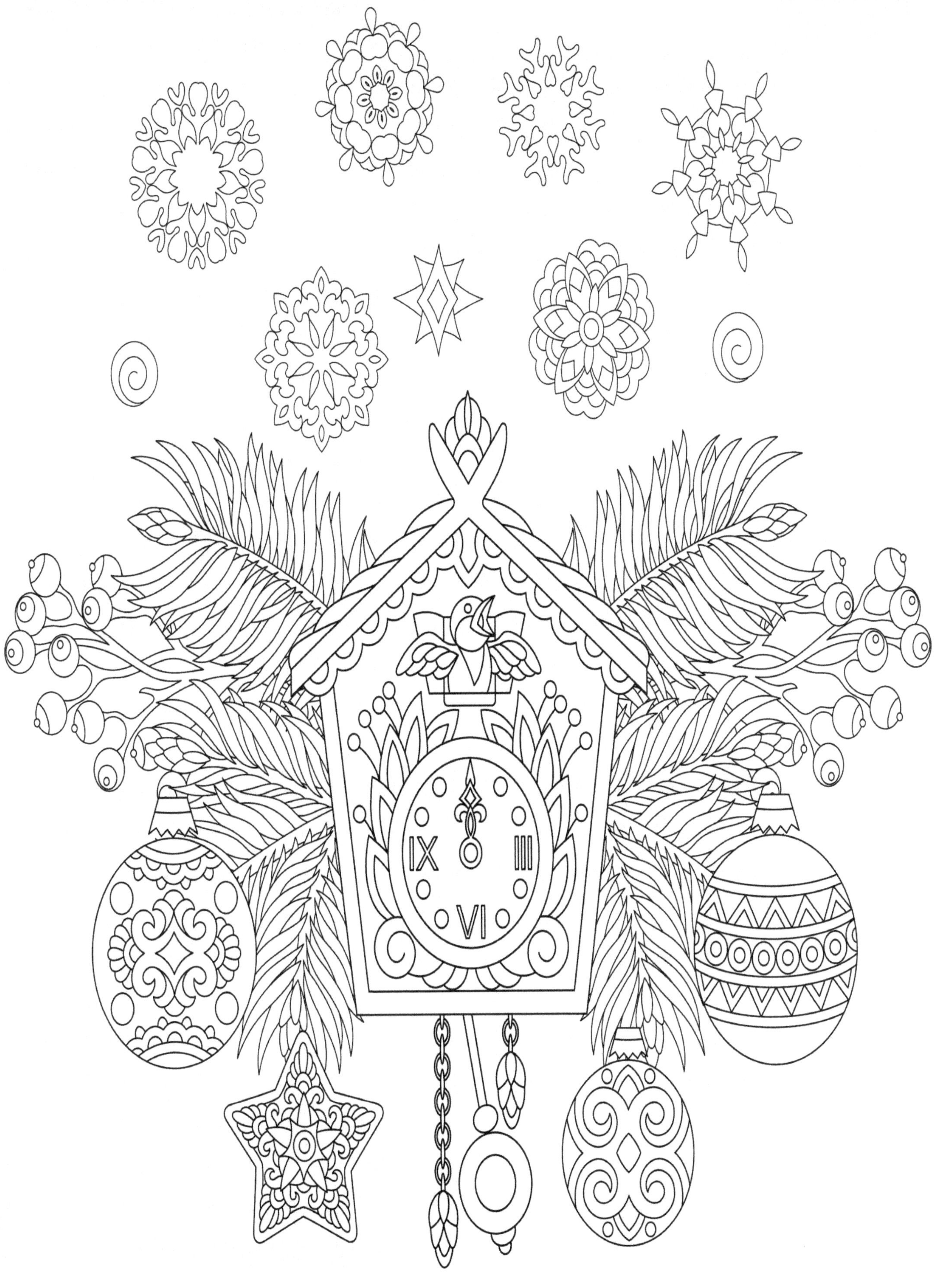

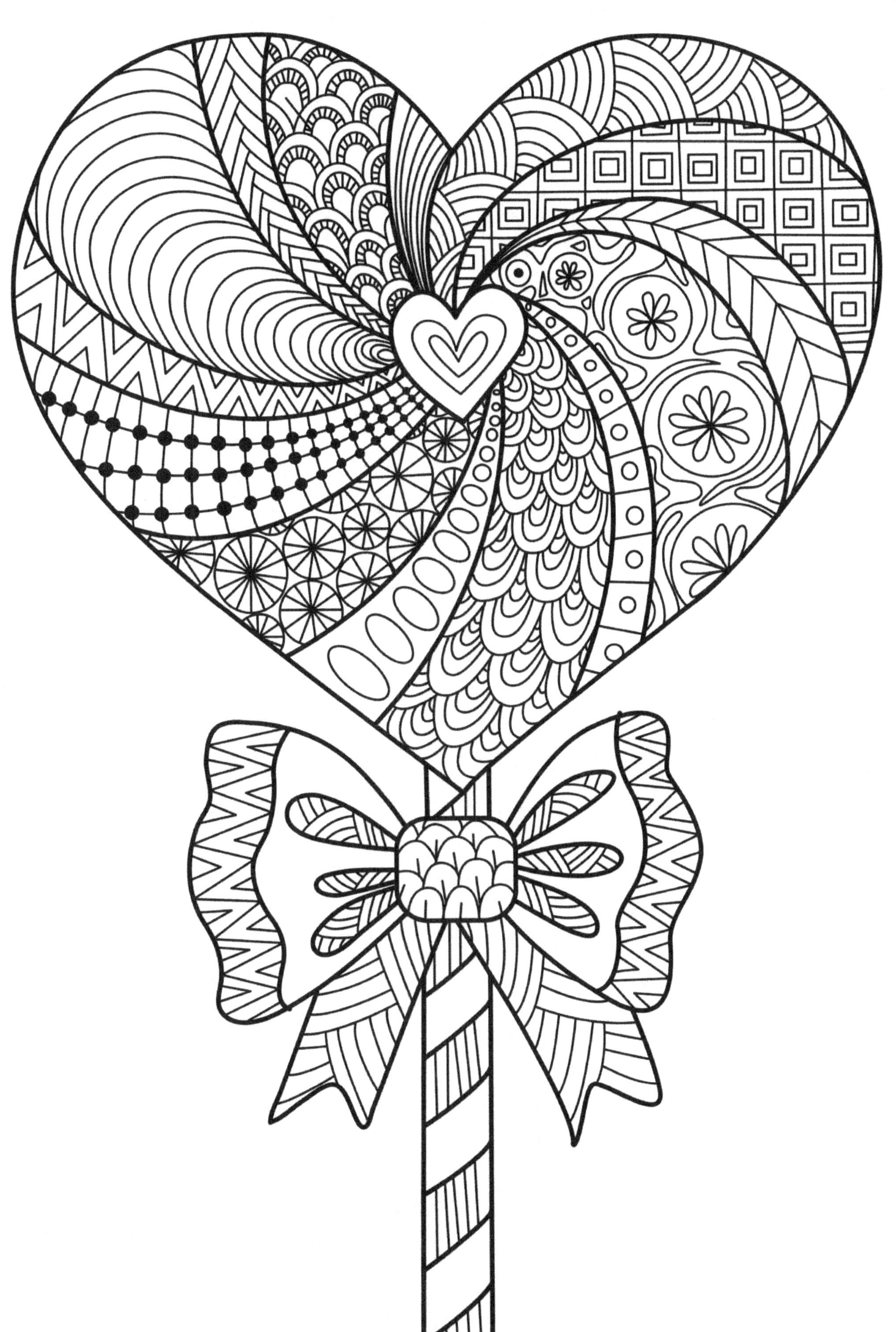

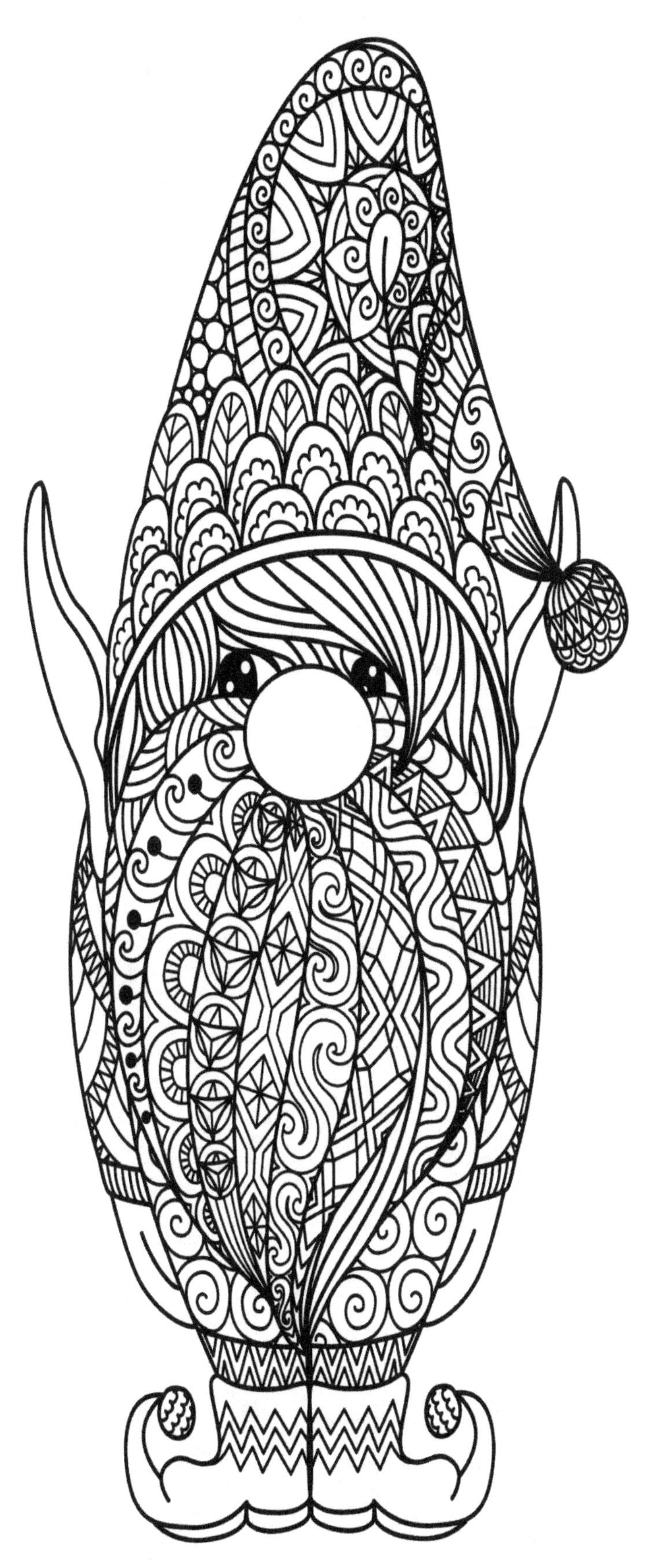

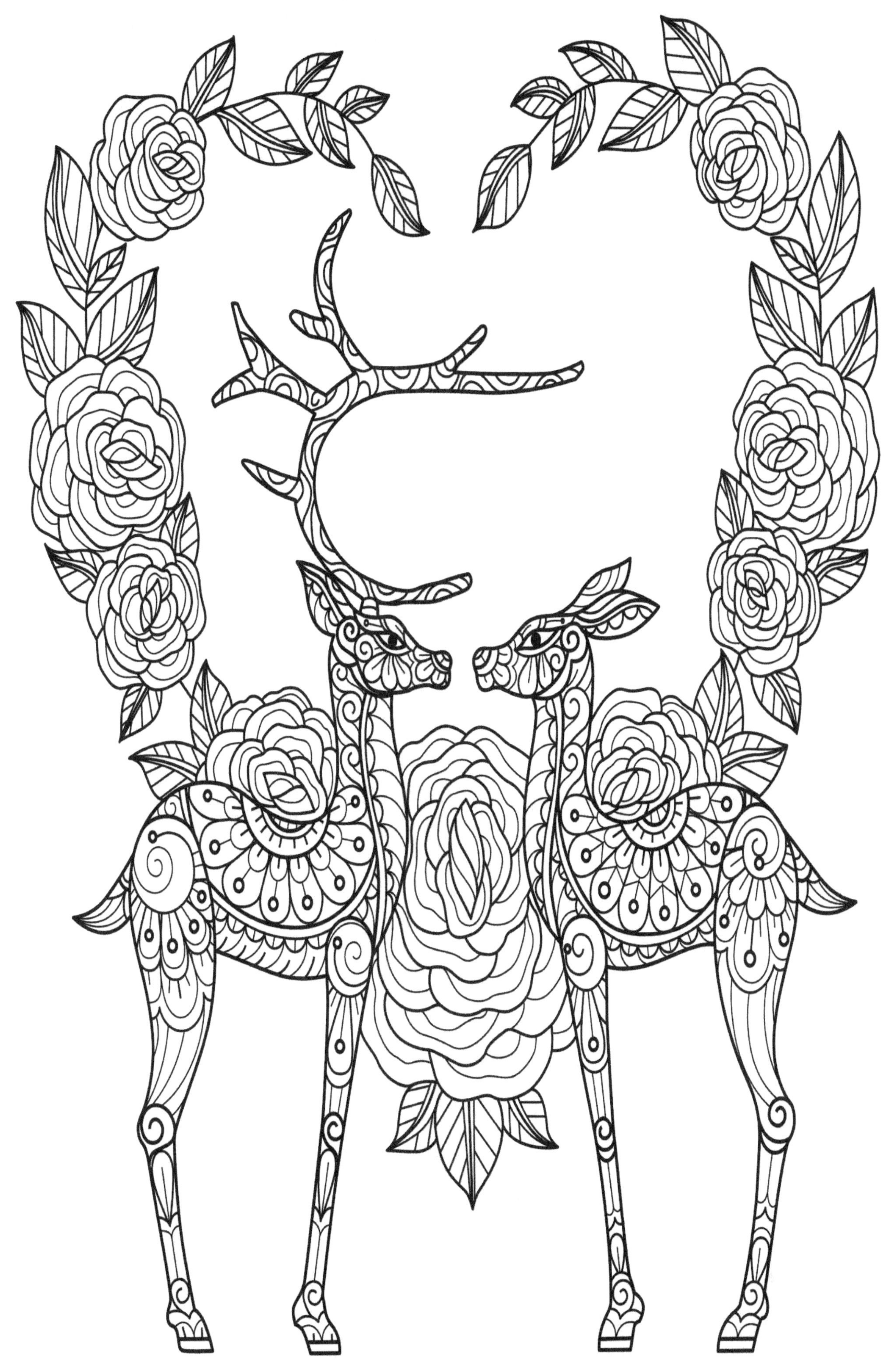

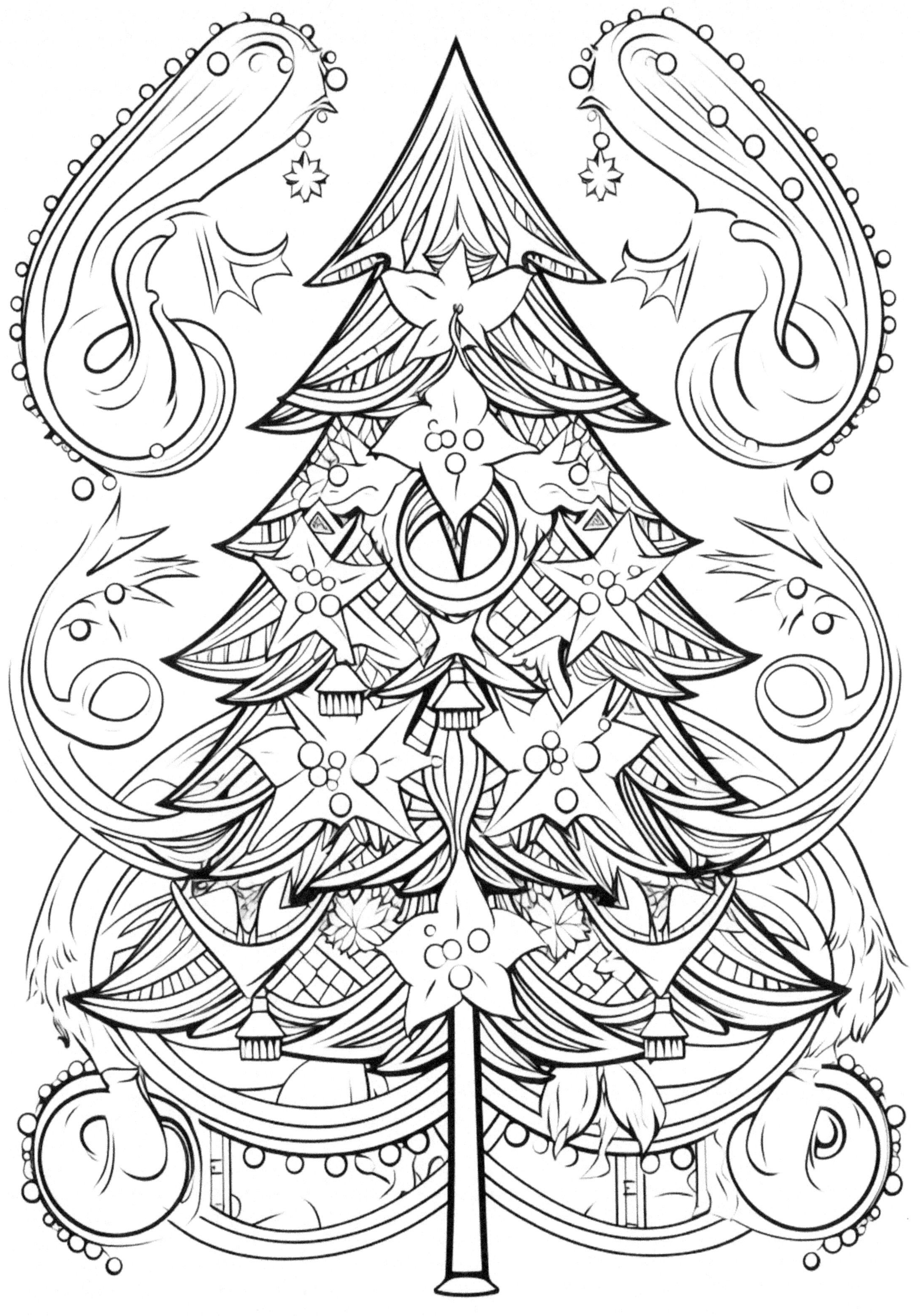

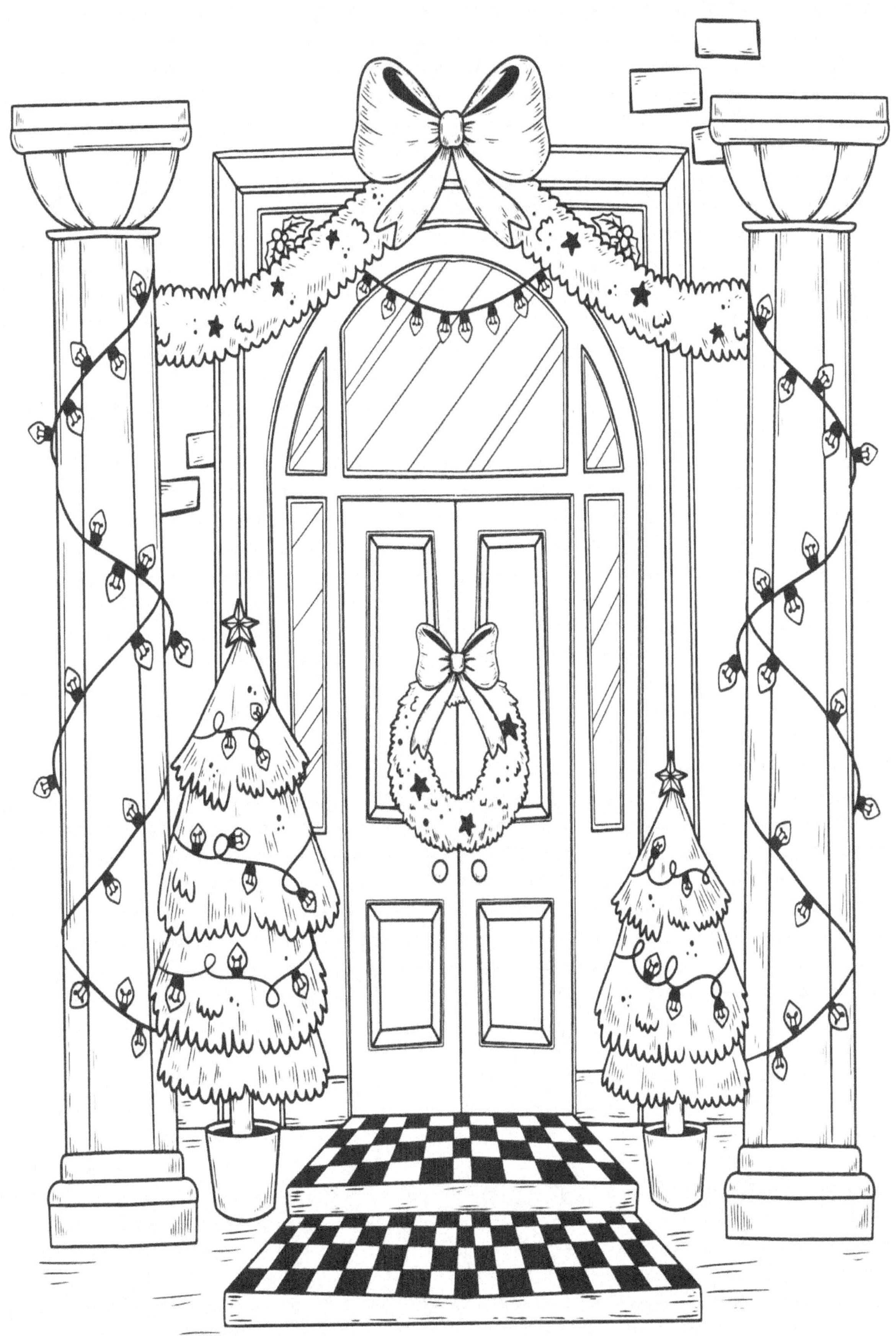

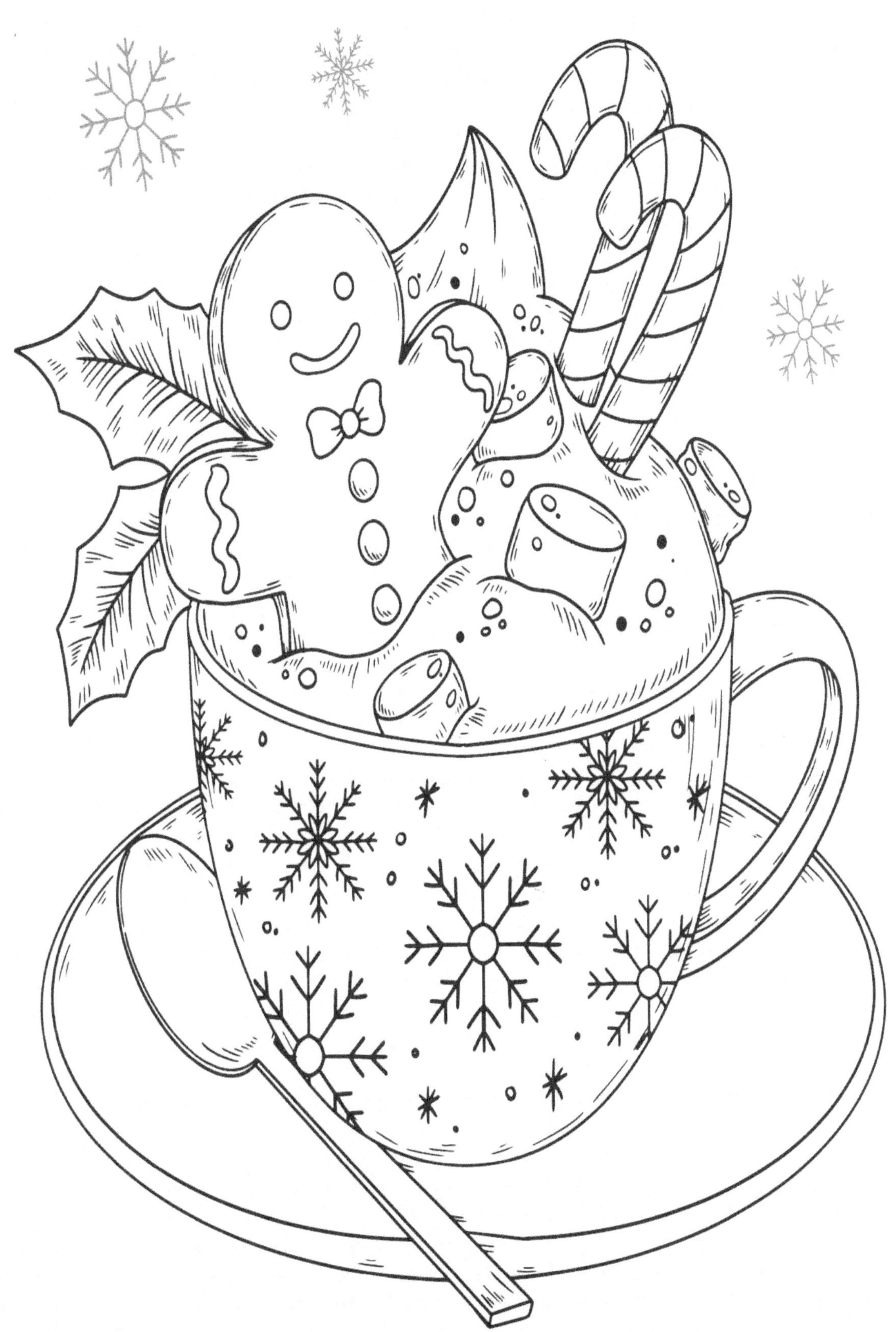

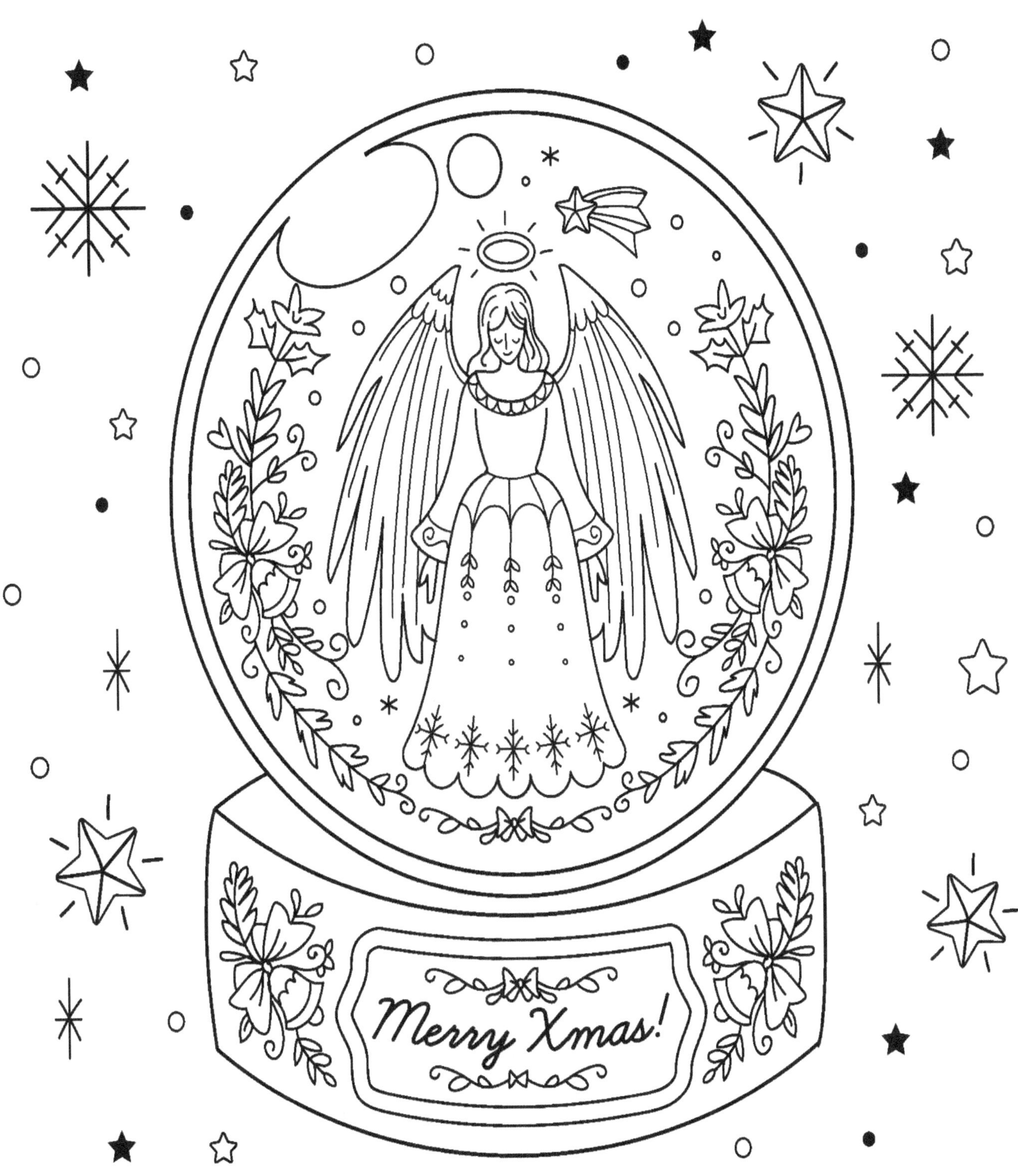
Merry Xmas!

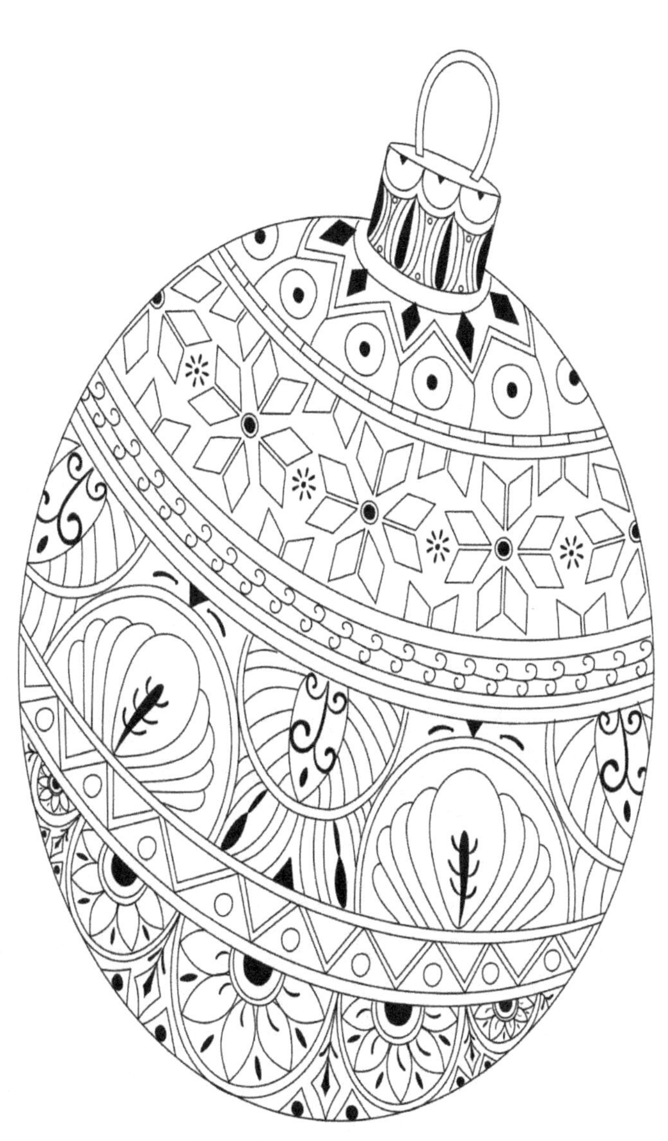

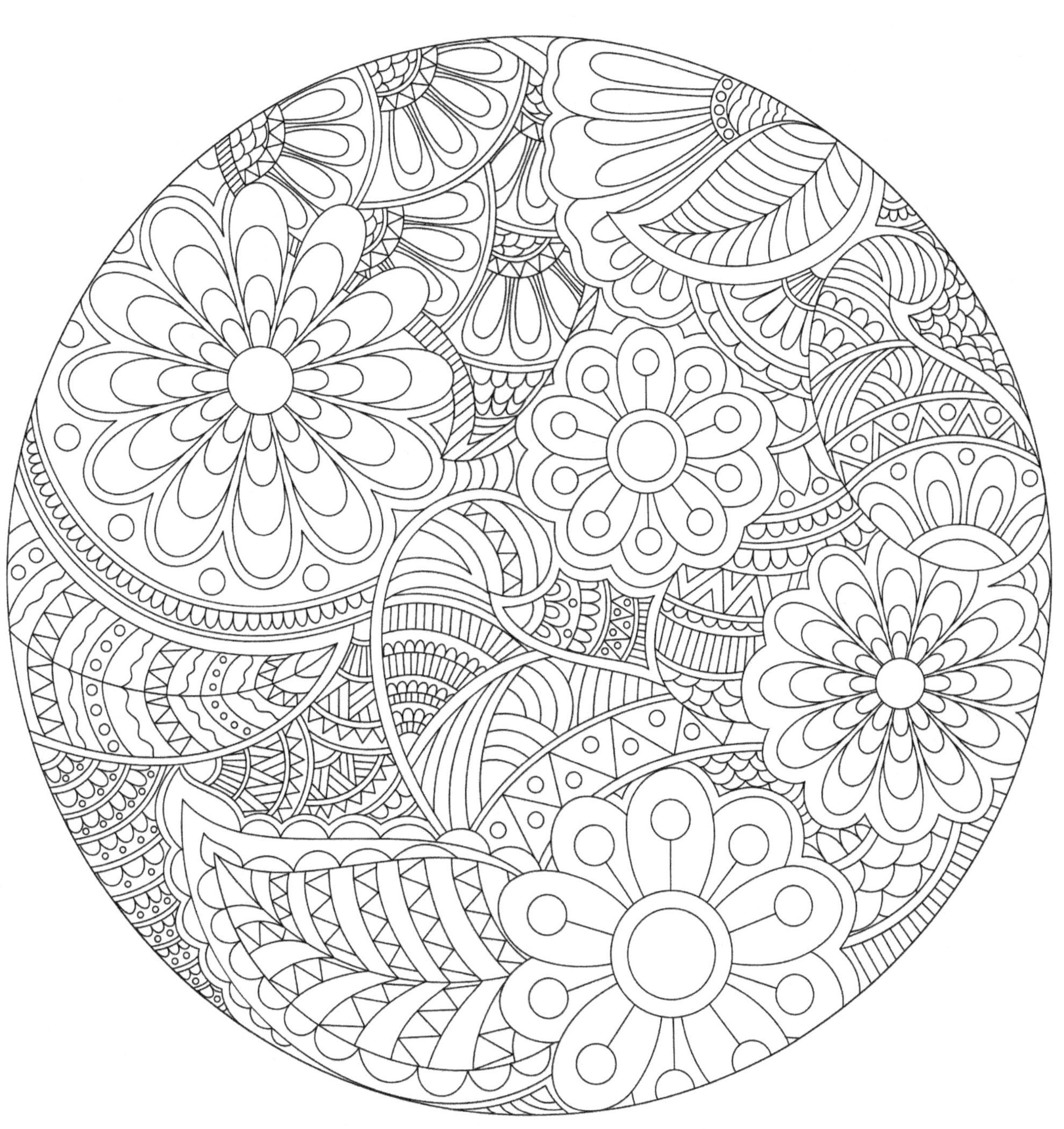

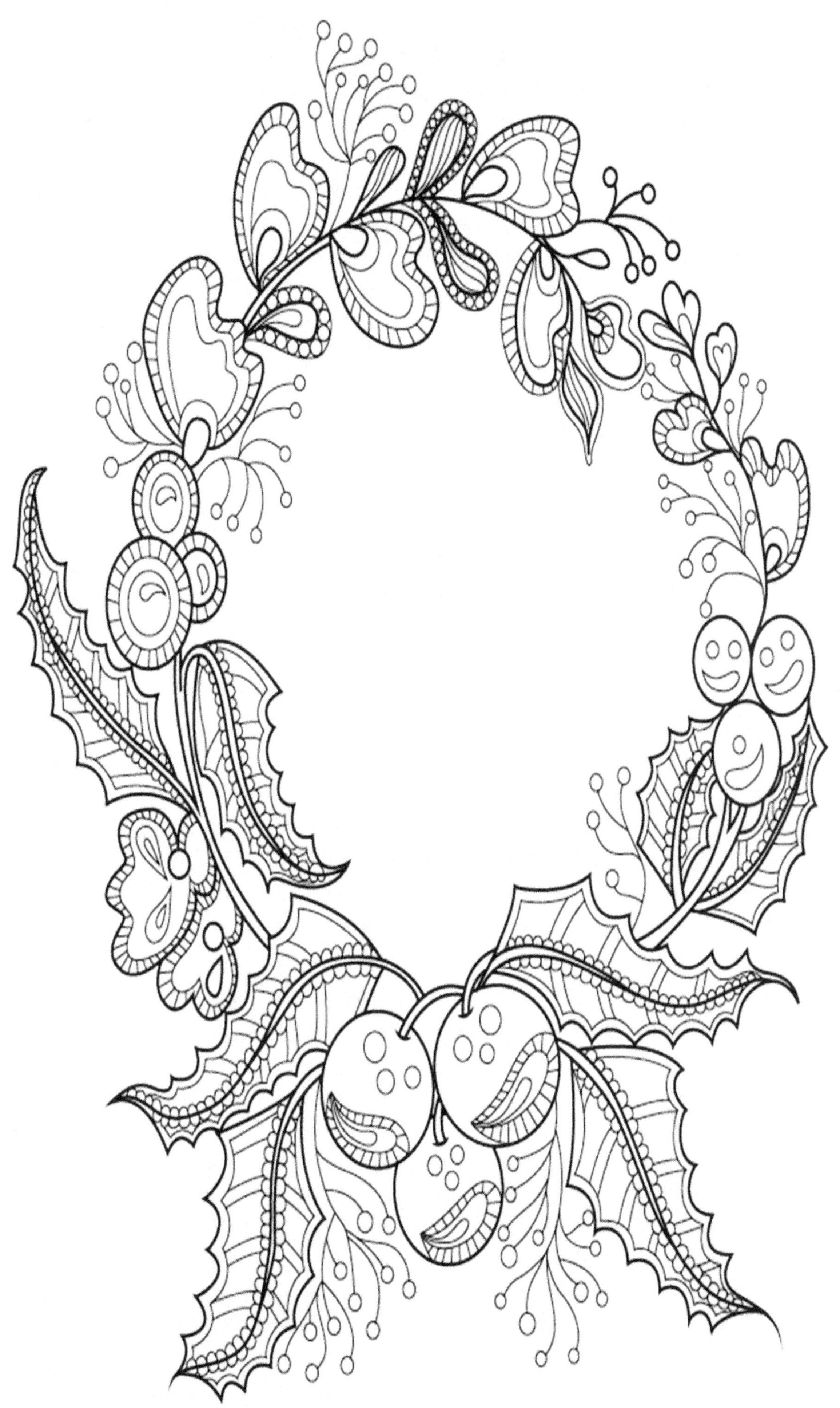

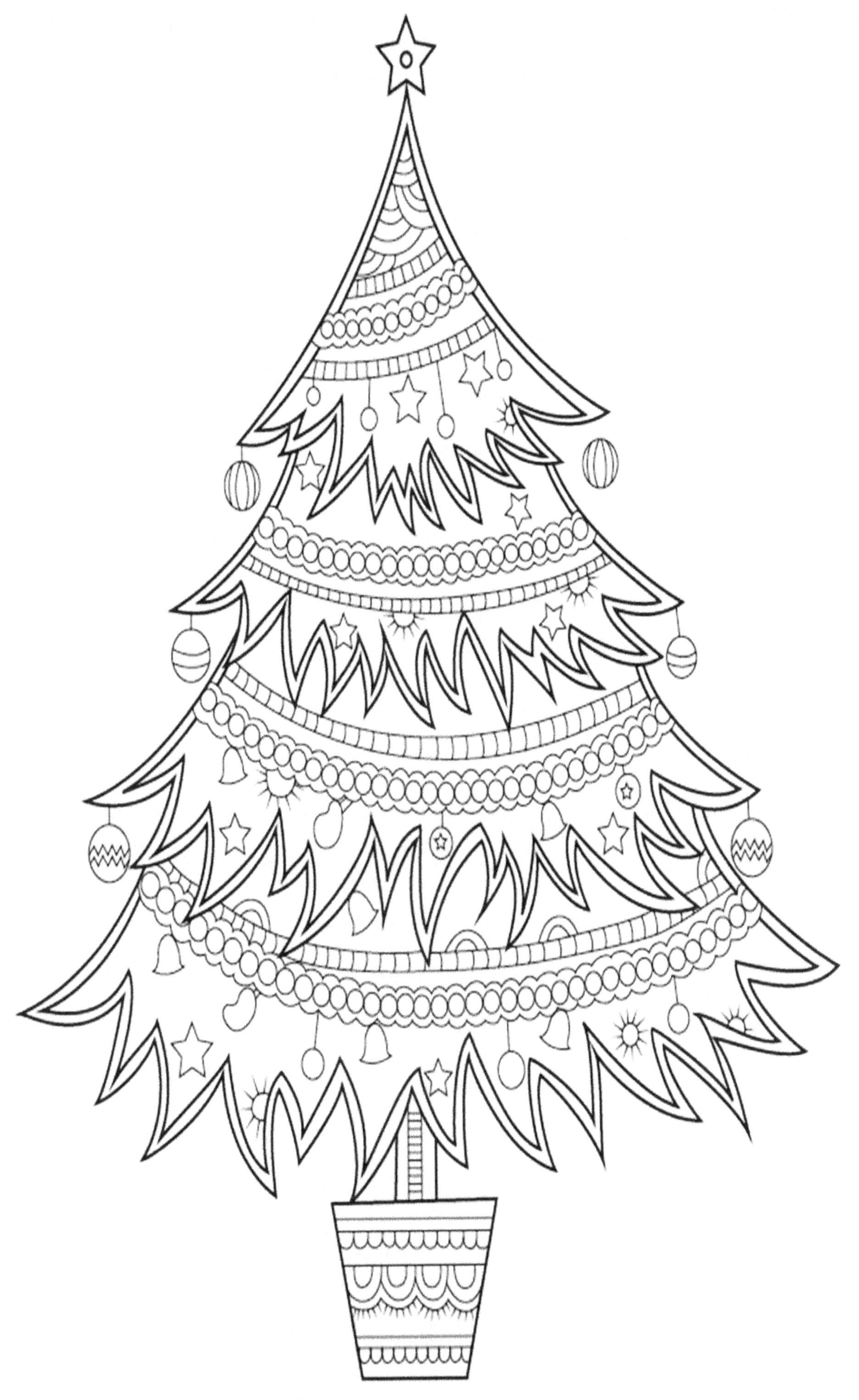

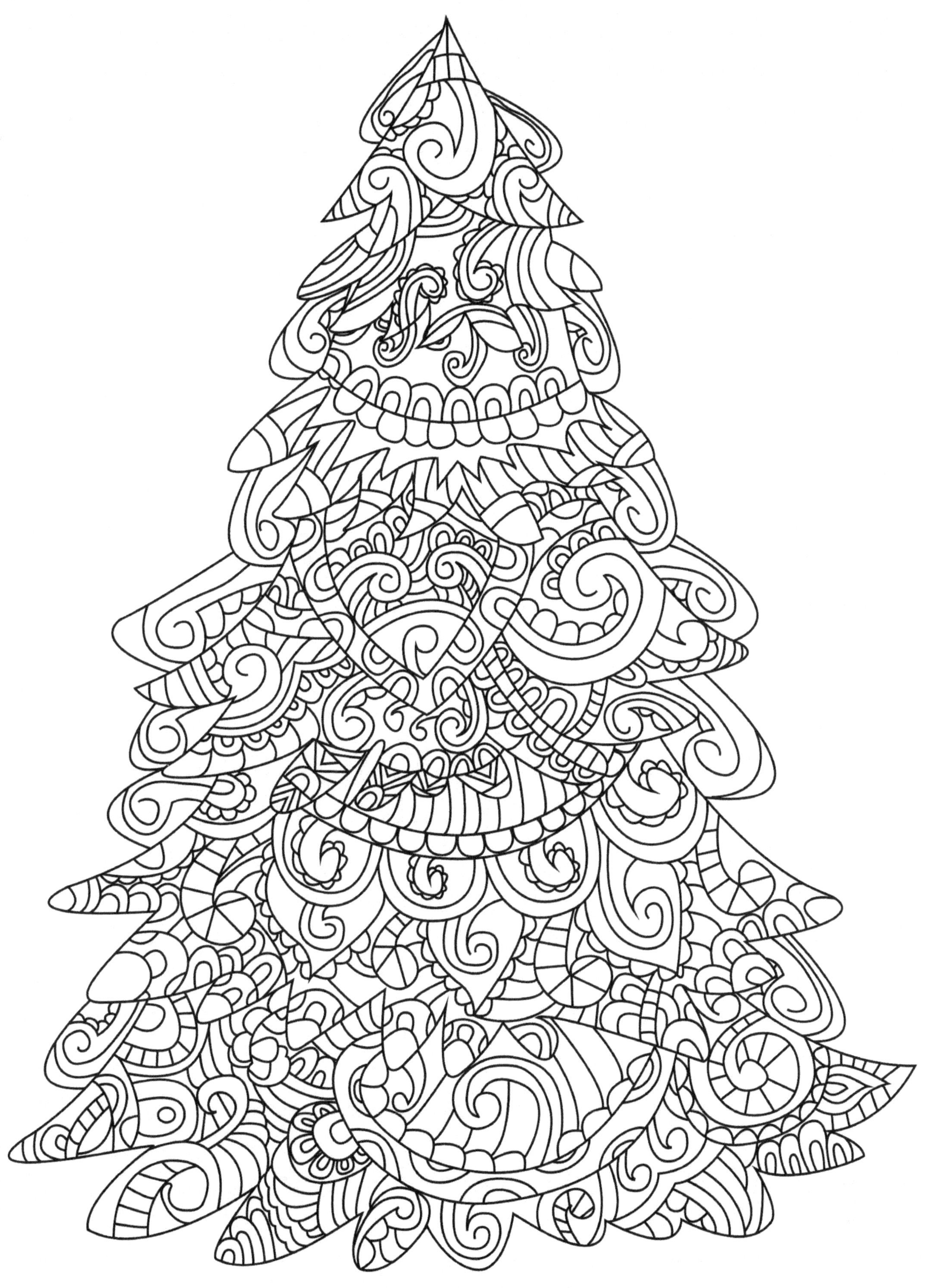

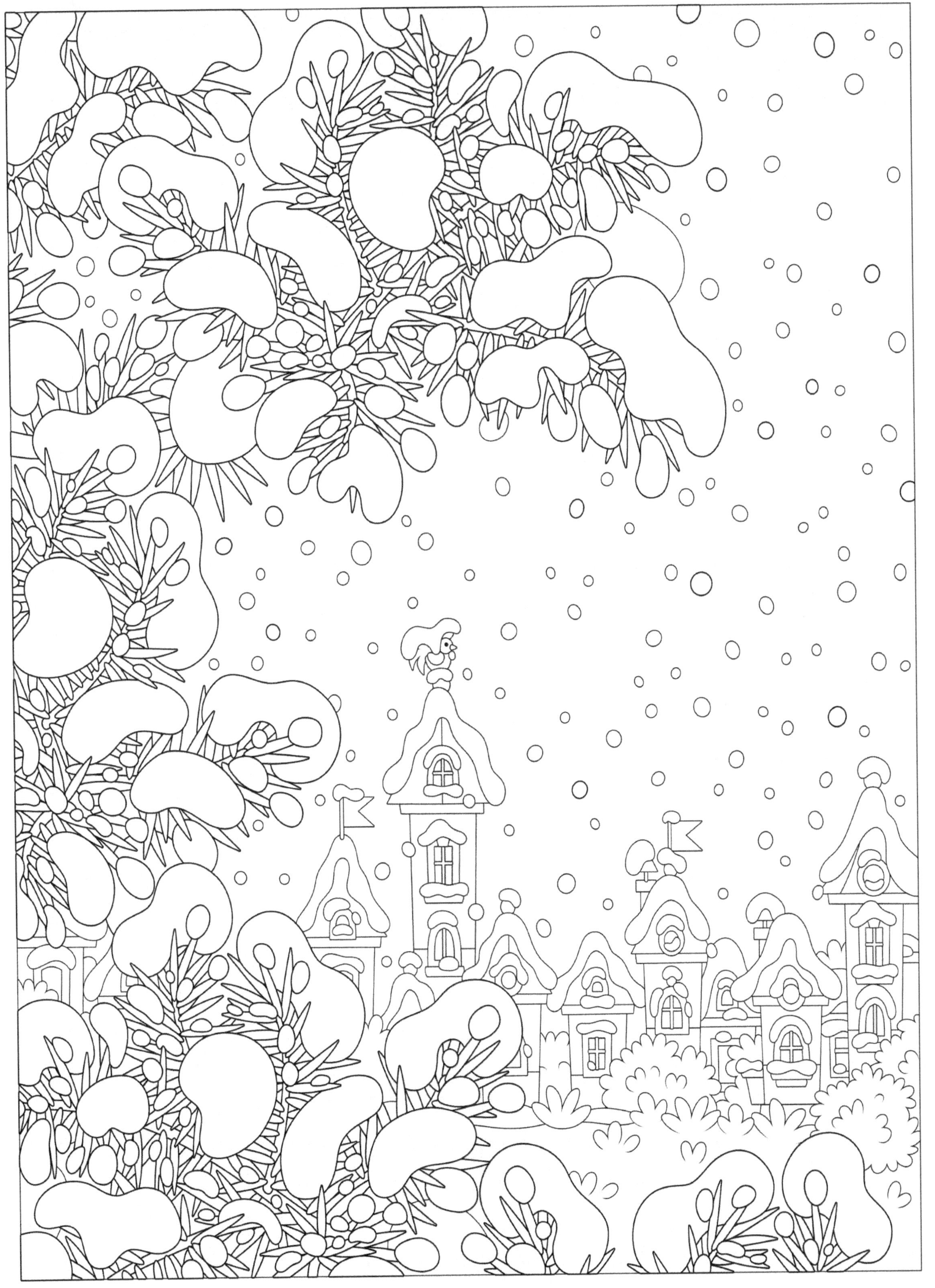

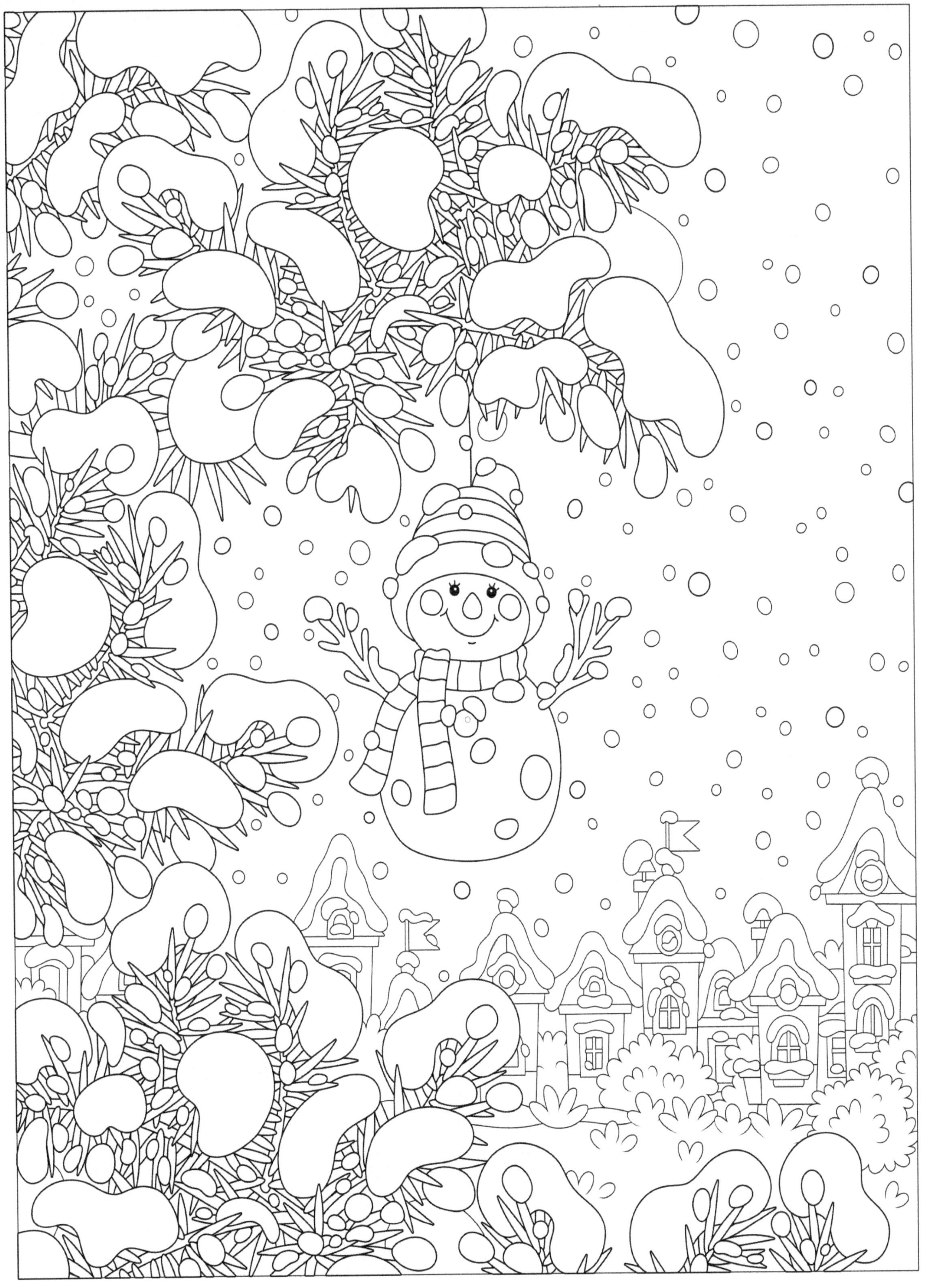

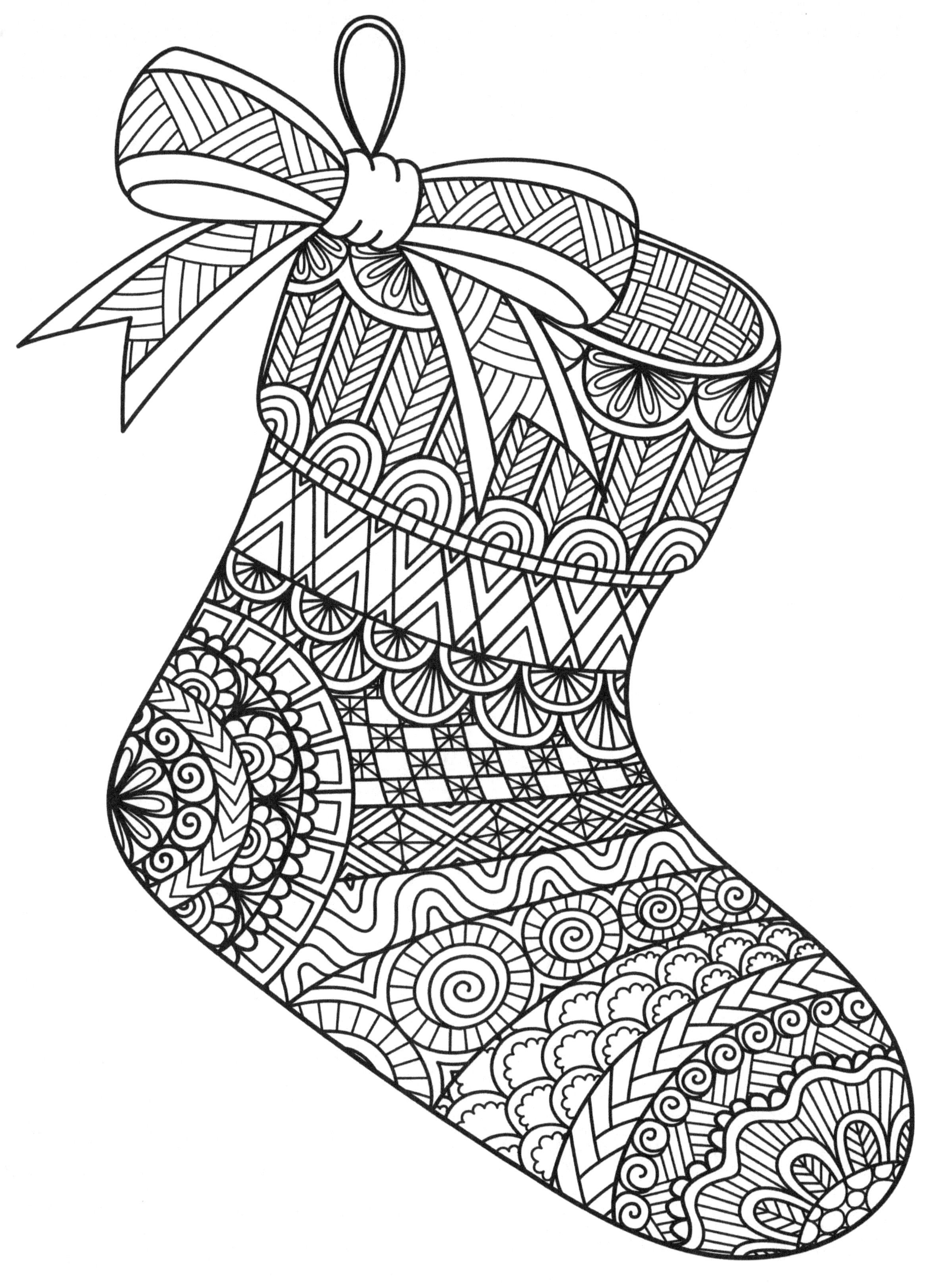

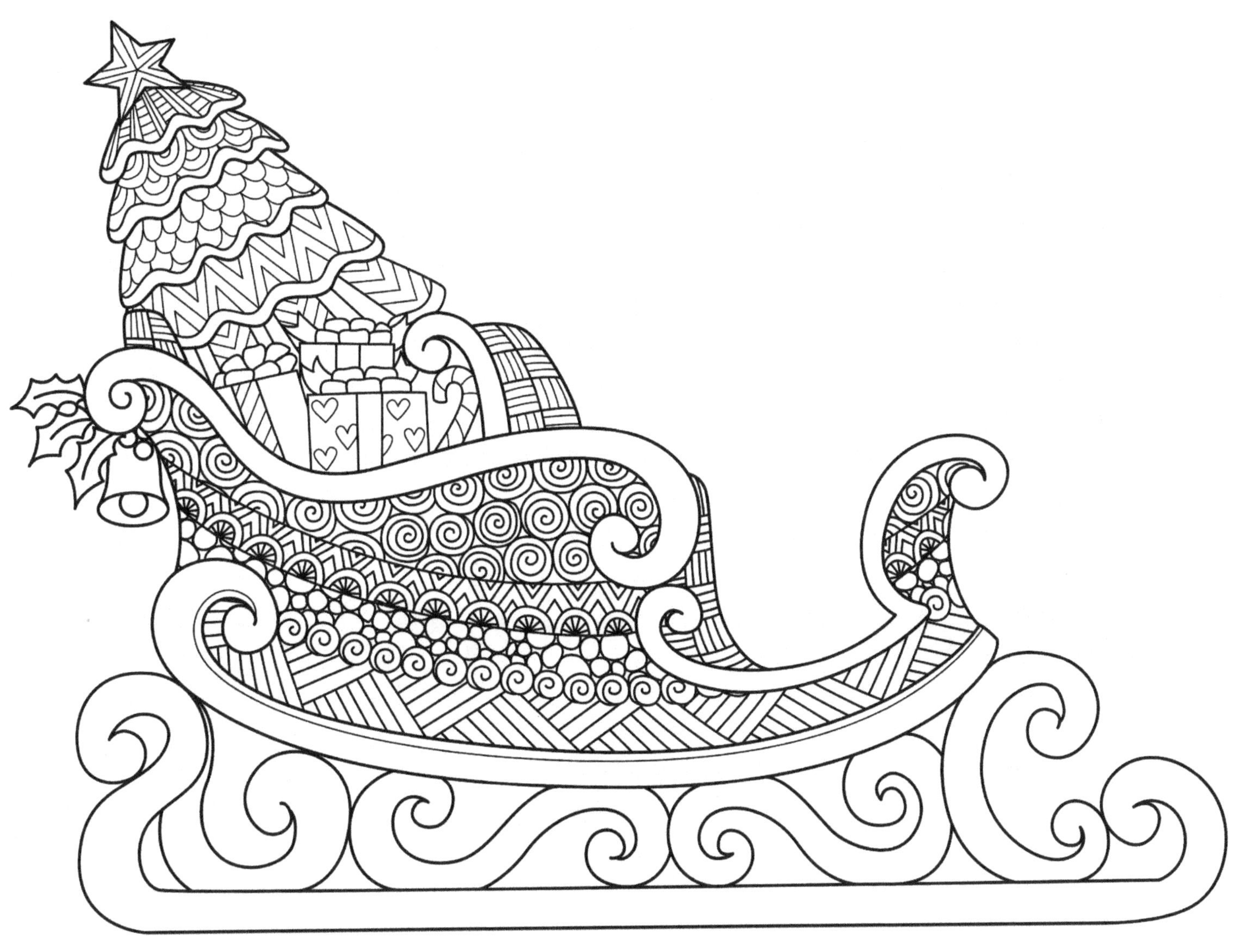

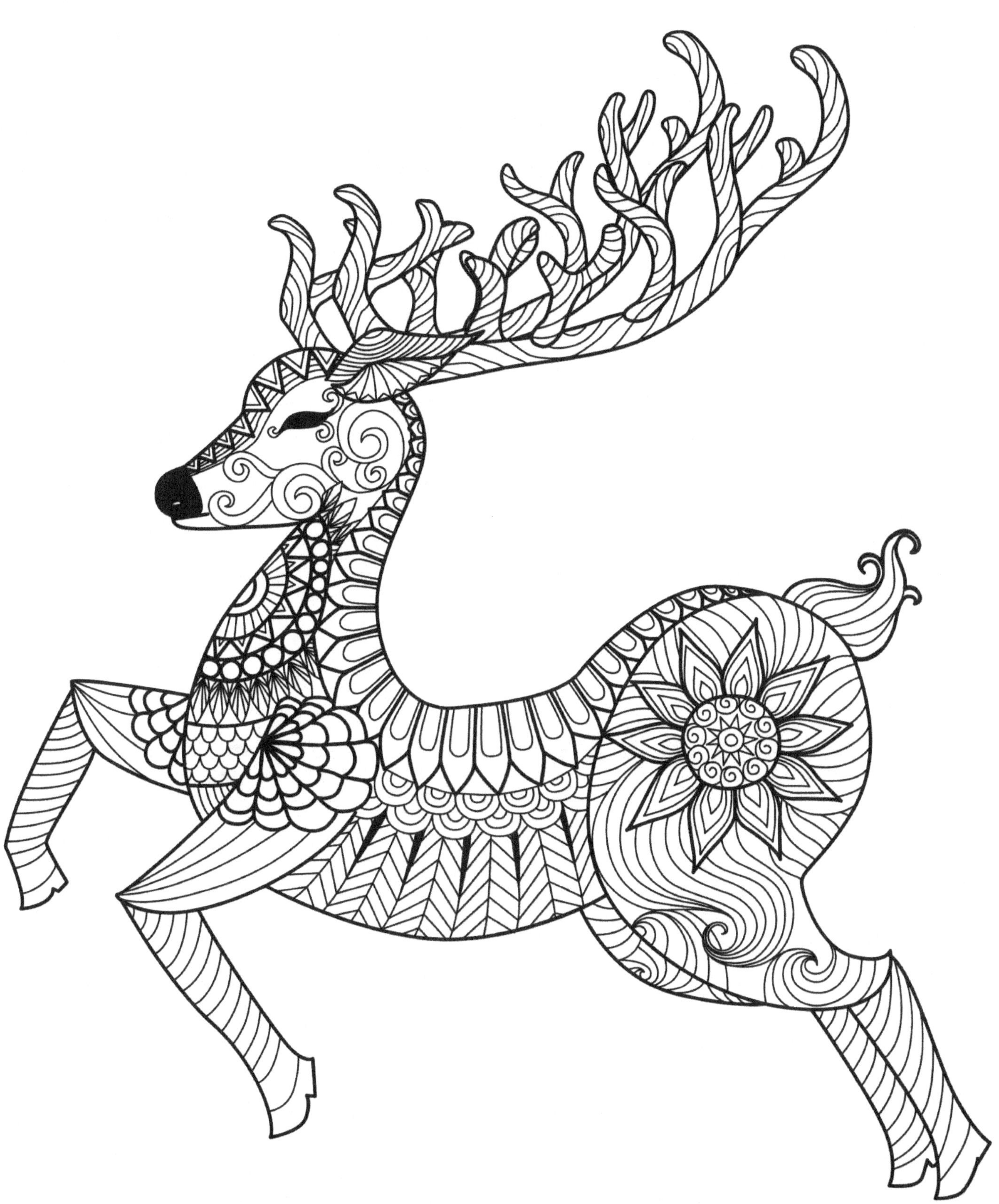

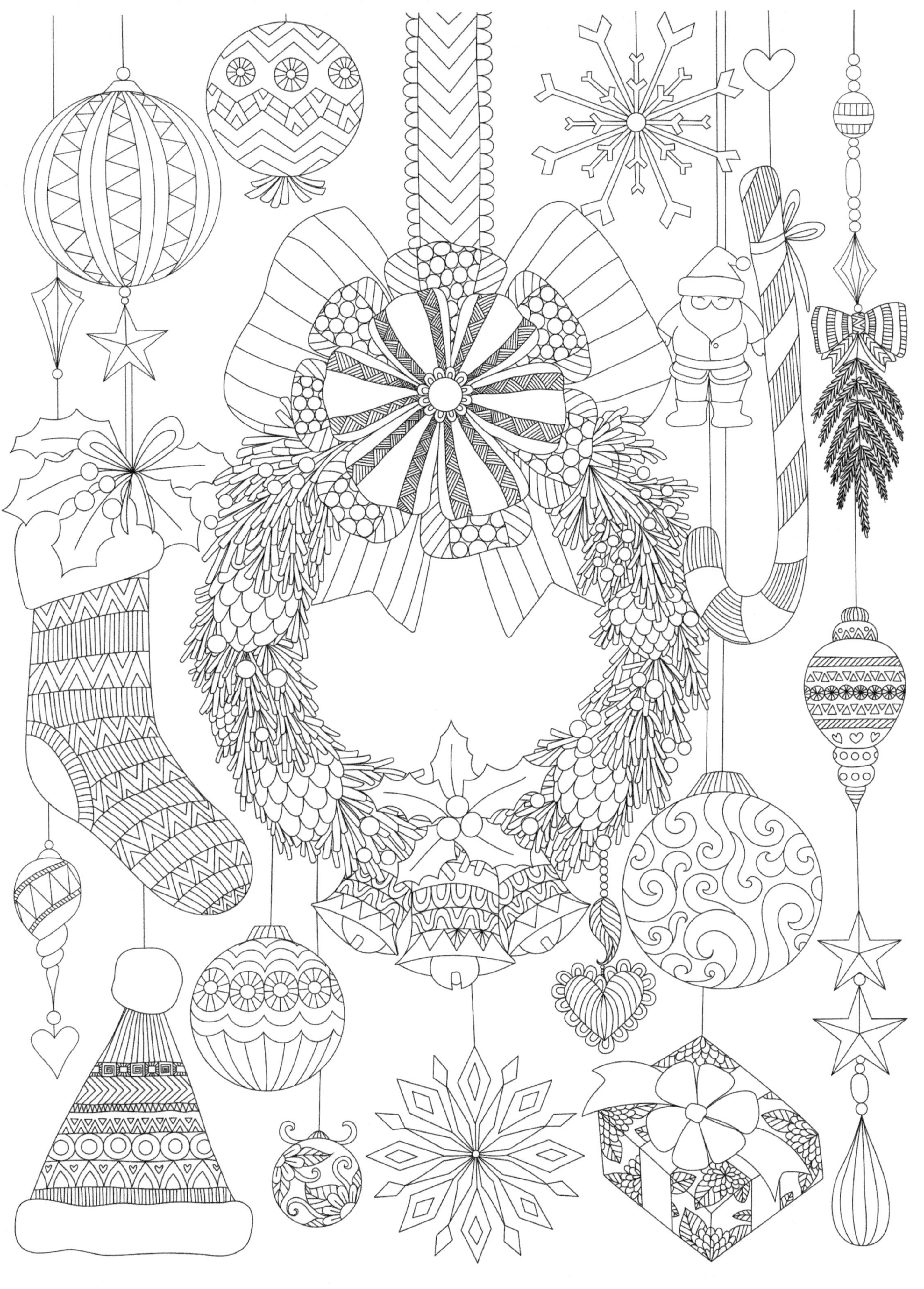

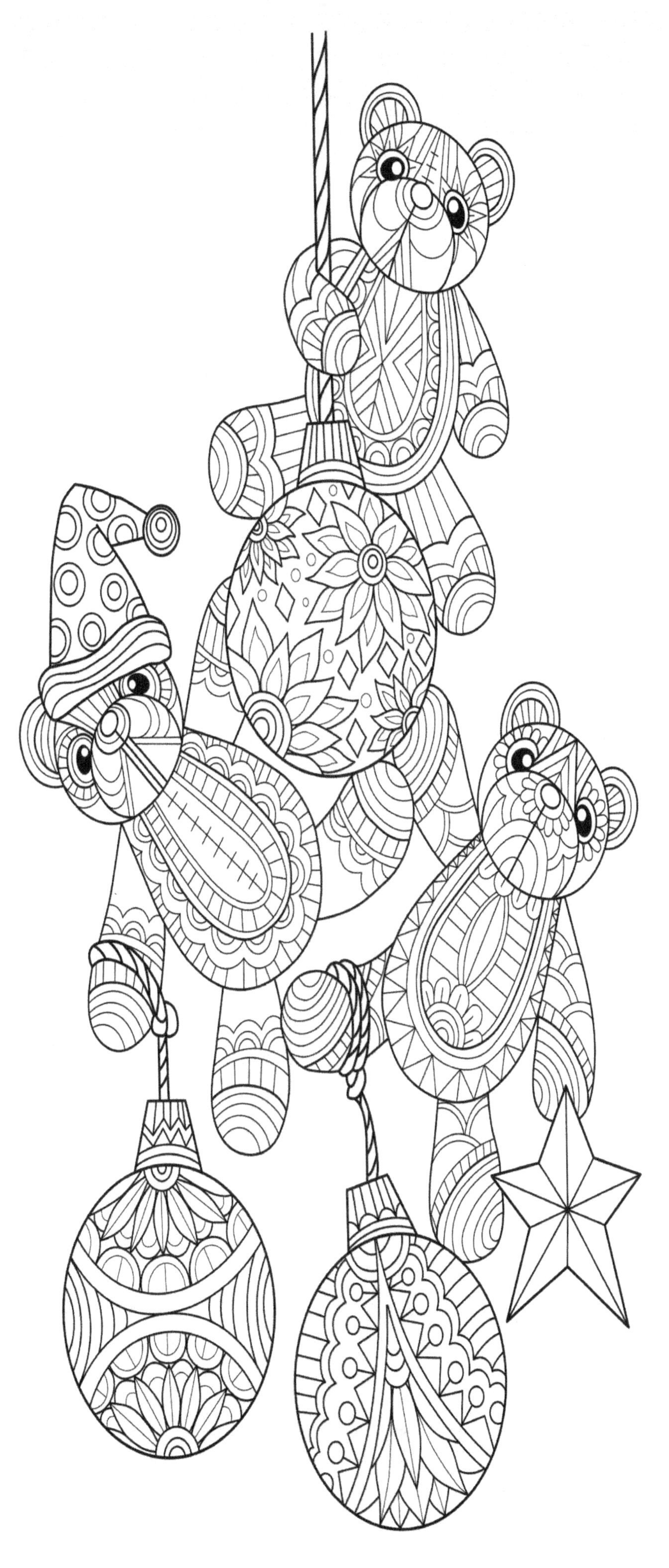

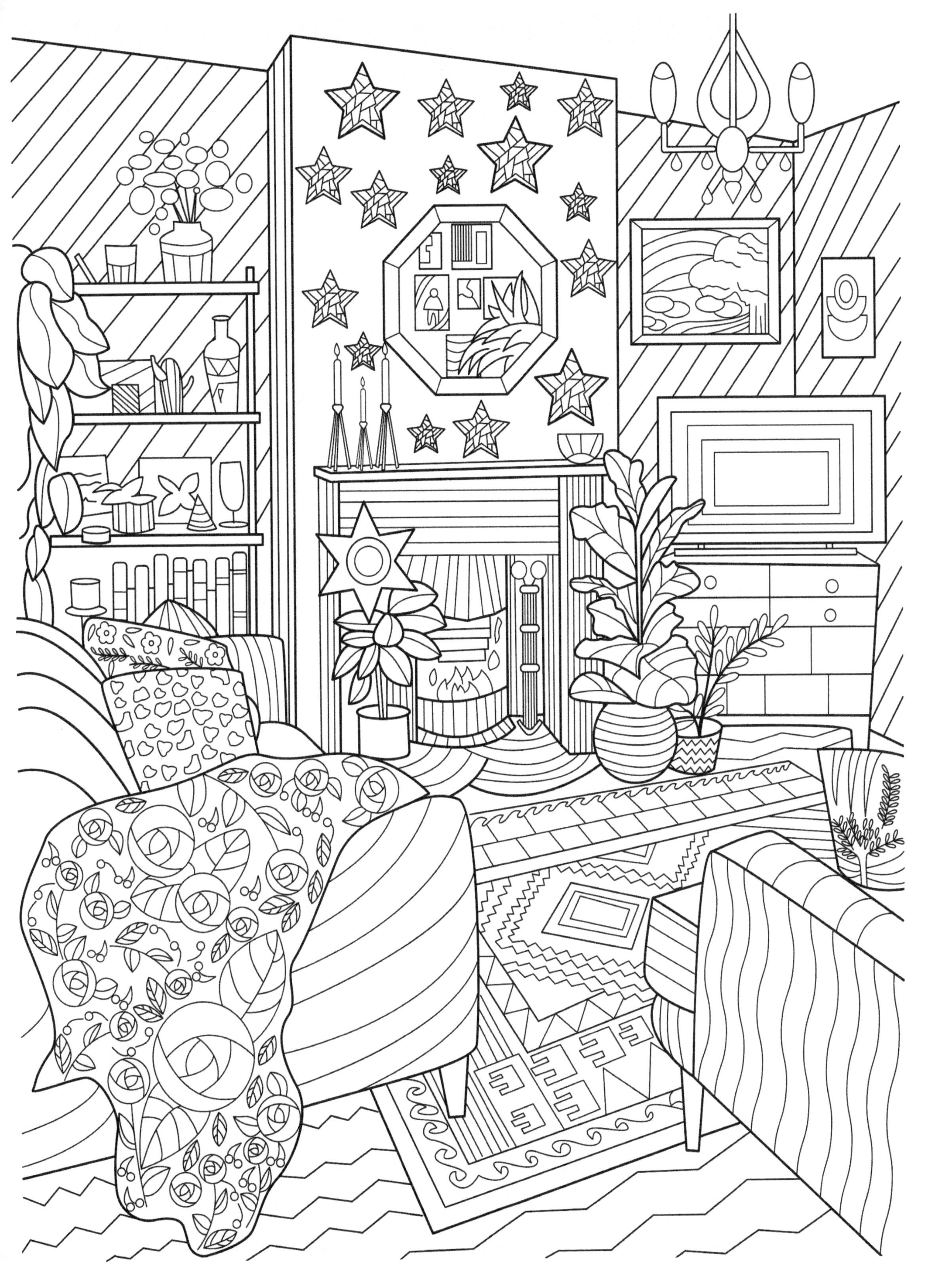

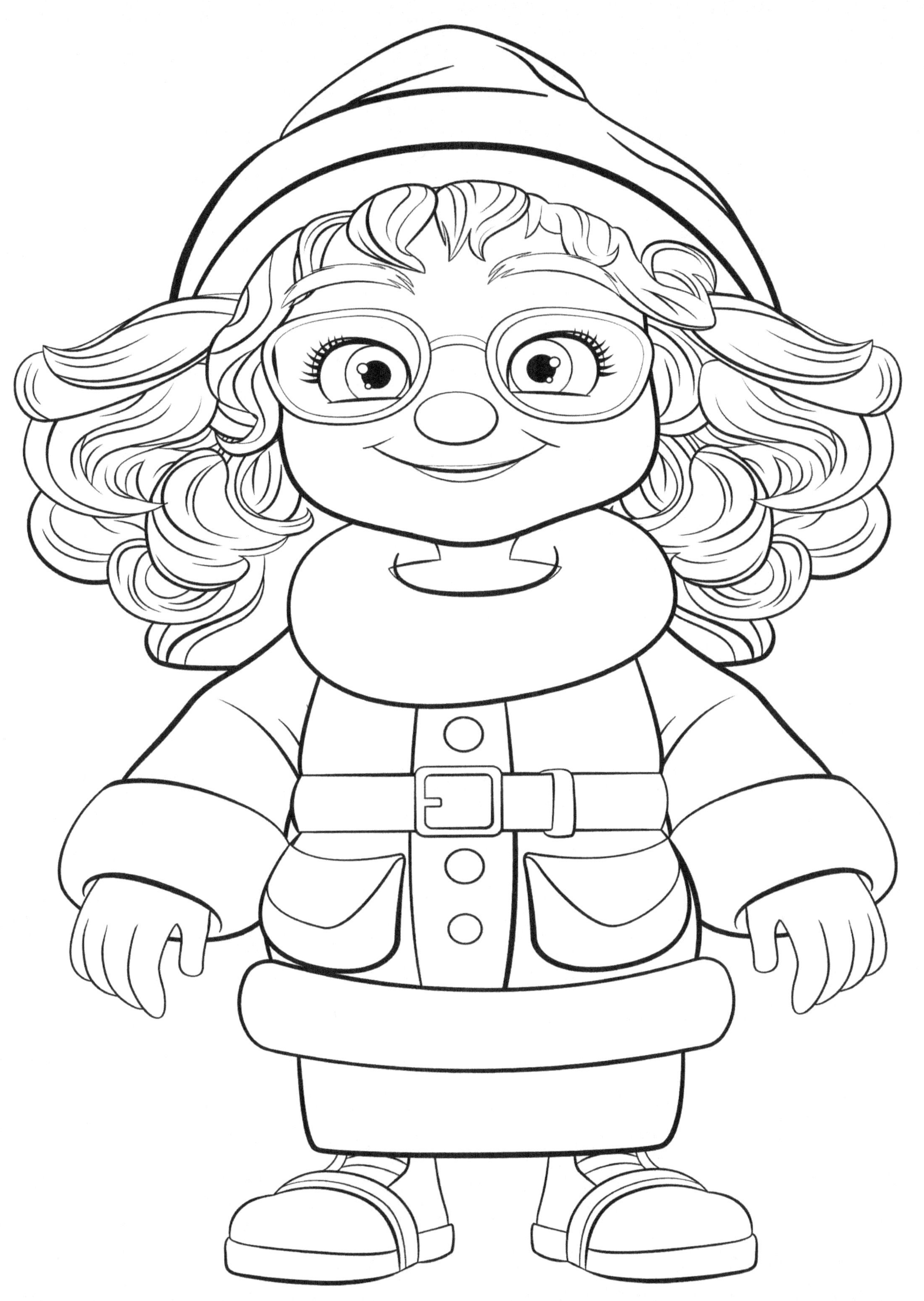

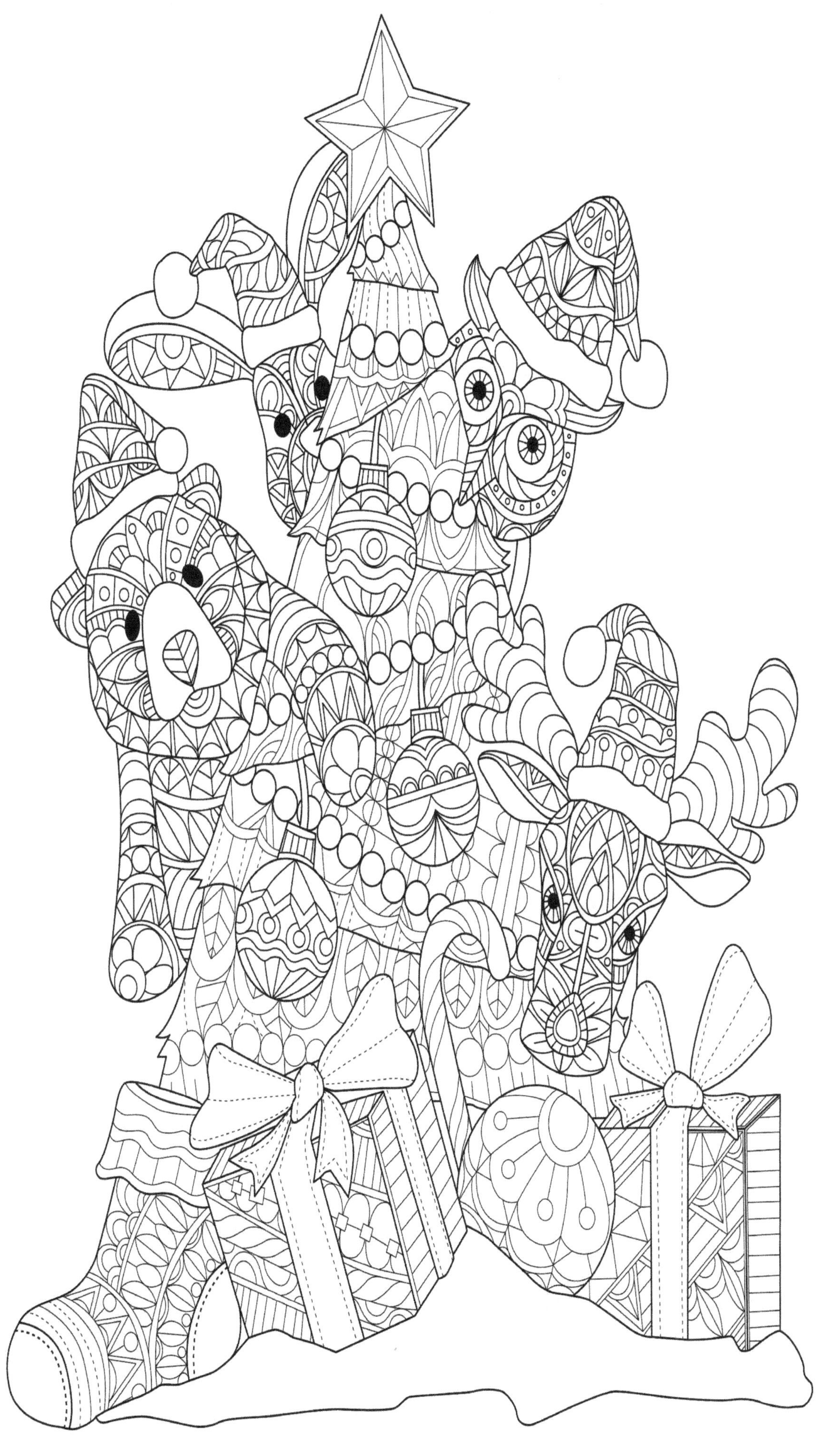